NO
BARRIER

Other Books Translated by Thomas Cleary

NO BARRIER

Unlocking the Zen Koan

A New Translation of the Zen Classic
Wumenguan
[Mumonkan]

Translated from the Chinese
and Commentary by

Thomas Cleary

BANTAM BOOKS
New York   Toronto   London   Sydney   Auckland

NO BARRIER

A Bantam Book / February 1993

All rights reserved.
Copyright © 1993 by Thomas Cleary.

BOOK DESIGN BY CAROL MALCOLM-RUSSO

Library of Congress Cataloging-in-Publication Data

Hui-k' ai, 1183–1260.
    [Wu-men kuan. English]
    No barrier : unlocking the Zen koan : a new translation of the Zen classic
Wumenguan (Mumonkan) / by Thomas Cleary.
      p. cm.
    ISBN 0-553-37138-X
    1. Koan—Early works to 1800. I. Cleary, Thomas F., 1949–   . II. Title.
BQ9289.H8413 1992
294.3′4—dc20   91-42172
                                         CIP

Published simultaneously in the United States and Canada

Bantam Books are published by Bantam Books, a division of Bantam Doubleday Dell
Publishing Group, Inc. Its trademark, consisting of the words "Bantam Books" and
the portrayal of a rooster, is Registered in U.S. Patent and Trademark Office and in
other countries. Marca Registrada. Bantam Books, 666 Fifth Avenue, New York,
New York 10103.

PRINTED IN THE UNITED STATES OF AMERICA

RRH   0 9 8 7 6 5 4 3 2 1

Contents

Introduction

No *Barrier* is a new translation of *Wumenguan,* a classic collection of comments on Chinese Zen koans, symbolic stories designed to map the Zen Buddhist way to enlightenment. Koans are the most sophisticated of Zen devices, yet they can be used effectively even by novices. This book unravels the secrets of the most popular collection of koans, revealing them as tools for opening up the inherent genius of the mind.

Zen awakening liberates the mind from the limitations and burdens of narrow views, dogmatic assumptions, and circular thinking habits. This is figuratively called "taking off the blinders and unloading the saddlebags," in reference to the process of shedding binding fixations and clarifying the mind, "becoming bare and untrammeled, radiantly bright."

Zen is the heart of Buddhism, which is traditionally likened to a chariot running on two wheels, wisdom and compassion. The combination of these two qualities is customarily symbolized by a lotus blooming in a fire, representing the freedom of the liberated mind in the midst of the mundane world, transforming ordinary experience into extraordinary enlightenment.

The soul of Zen wisdom is called the heart of nirvana,

which is the quintessential realization of dispassionate objectivity. The spirit of Zen compassion is called knowledge of differentiation, because it is based on objective knowledge of the world. In symbolic language, the experience of nirvana is called the Land of Eternal Silent Light, while the experience of knowledge of the world is called the Land of True Reward.

The harmonious union and pragmatic coalescence of these two domains of experience, Silent Light and True Reward, is the means by which complete human fulfillment in this life on earth is approached in Zen Buddhism.

The Land of Eternal Silent Light and the Land of True Reward are both symbolic and descriptive of the nature of the experiences of the two sides of enlightenment. The Land of Eternal Silent Light is the domain of essence, or what we have always been; the Land of True Reward is the domain of function, or what we can possibly be. Eternal Silent Light is the wellspring of uninhibited wisdom; True Reward is the wellspring of uninhibited compassion.

All of the Zen koans in this collection represent mental exercises for the realization of these experiences and their ultimate integration and mature development in complete consciousness. Some koans, beginning with the first, focus primarily on Silent Light or ways of arriving there; others, beginning with the second koan, focus primarily on True Reward or ways of arriving there. The most advanced koans also give techniques of integration, as do the traditional Zen commentaries on koans.

The *Wumenguan* is one of seven major Chinese collections of comments on Zen koans. It was compiled over seven hundred and fifty years ago by a distinguished Chinese Zen master, whose comments in verse and prose illumine the inner meaning of the koans.

Formally the briefest, simplest, and most succinct of

the major collections, the *Wumenguan* is popularly regarded as the most accessible of classical koan studies. To the Zen eye, however, the brevity and simplicity of its format do not indicate a rudimentary level of sophistication, but the very opposite. The text is perhaps the most intensely concentrated, and therefore supremely economical, presentation of the fullest ranges of Zen teaching that can be suggested in words.

The extraordinary density of meaning achieved in the *Wumenguan* can be glimpsed in the multiplicity of ideas conveyed in the title alone, which not only identifies the text but also describes the nature of its contents and function, and thus the purpose of its existence.

The first obvious way to read the original title *Wumenguan* is "Wumen's Border Pass." Wumen is one of the names by which the Chinese Zen master who authored the text is known. Wumen Huikai (pronounced Woo-mun Hway-kai) lived from 1183 to 1260. His own preface to *Wumenguan* is dated 1228, so Wumen's comments on the koans were delivered at the age of forty-five, when he was in the prime of life.

A Zen master in a classical book or story is not just a historical person, but also symbolizes some aspect of Zen. Huikai, Wumen's original Buddhist name, means "Ocean of Wisdom." He acquired the name Wumen, "The Gate of No," due to his long practice of a powerful Zen exercise (taught in the first koan) to which this name also refers, as explained below.

The "Border Pass" in the title as read in this manner refers to the koans themselves, and to the process of unlocking and actualizing koans. Your understanding of the koans is your own passport across the border of mental barriers, your passage into mental freedom.

Another way to read the title *Wumenguan* is "The Border Pass Whose Doorway is *No.*" This meaning refers to a basic Zen practice and experience, which may be described as radical disentanglement from thought and conceptualization. Here, *No* symbolizes a cornerstone of Buddhist logic as well as a fundamental Zen exercise. The logical principle is that no human conception can grasp absolute reality as it is in itself. The Zen exercise is that taught in the first koan, one by which the mind transcends subjective biases and acquired conceptions of the world, thereby arriving at direct witness of reality.

The title *Wumenguan* can also be read, "The Barrier That Has No Door," or "The Bolt on a Nonexistent Door." These meanings allude to the Zen teaching that the human mind is unnecessarily imprisoned by barriers of habit, mechanical patterns of thought and activity, routines that seem real and true only because they engage the best of our attention. Zen demonstrates the objective unreality of conceptual barriers to objective perception; the koans are a means of breaking through these mental barriers to allow the mind's eye to see through the veil of illusion to actual truth.

The title *Wumenguan* also means "There Is No Door Bolt." According to the central teaching of Buddhism, in reality nothing cloisters the mind but attachment to its own thoughts and projections. The meaning of Zen is to realize this fact in experience, in the experience of genuine freedom of mind. Thus, summing up the essential meanings, I have translated the title as *No Barrier* to represent the philosophy, practice, and realization of Zen as taught through the koans in this famous collection.

ZEN AND KOAN STUDY

Koan-based Zen follows the order of spiritual practice taught by Jesus: "Seek the Kingdom of God first: then all things will be added." Returning to the symbolic terms introduced at the outset, it can be said that the

Zen Buddhist using koans first seeks the experience of the Land of Eternal Silent Light, then from there attains direct, firsthand knowledge of the Land of True Reward. The order and content of the first and second koans in No Barrier reflect this design, setting the fundamental pattern for working through the entire collection.

It is axiomatic that the awakening experiences and direct perceptions of Zen realization cannot be explained or understood as they really are by means of intellectual interpretation or conceptual thought, because they are not in the domain of ideation. For this reason, no theoretical discussion of koans will convey the genuine enlightenment of Zen. In order to benefit from the use of koans, it is necessary to employ them for the purpose and in the manner for which they were designed. To get the most out of this book, therefore, it is imperative to use it with the whole mind, both reading the koans and performing the indicated mental exercises.

Because of the pragmatic nature of koans, there is no substitute for getting directly involved with them. The following method of using this book is based on koan techniques articulated approximately one thousand years ago in the Zen tradition taught by Wumen. These techniques range from elementary initiatory methods for practical introduction to Zen experience, all the way to integrative methods of attaining the highest ranges of Zen realization.

APPLYING ZEN KOANS

The most basic traditional application of a Zen koan has two aspects. First is the simple act of calling a koan to mind from time to time, in all sorts of situations. Persistent repetition of this practice fosters the ability to engage an extra dimension of attention at will, a capacity that can be useful for enhancing general effectiveness in life through increasing the scope and fluidity of awareness.

The second aspect of this basic koan practice is developed and fortified in the process of calling koans to attention. As the mind gradually becomes steeped in the pattern of the koans, they reveal themselves as guides to specific exercises in Zen perspective and perception. Now the power of mental command developed in the first stage of deliberate recollection of koans is applied to consciously exercising the special perspectives represented by the koans.

Many people have found it useful to stand, sit, walk, or lie in a very quiet state while trying to solidify their koan recollection or perspective, but to really master Zen it is imperative to develop the capacity to practice Zen in the course of all activities. One of the major functions of koan practice is to empower Zen in action, so that the development of higher consciousness can continue uninterrupted regardless of whether there is calm or disturbance in your thoughts or surroundings. This is the beauty and grace of koans, one of the underlying reasons for their perennial attraction.

The first two koans in this collection afford the most basic illustrations of the meeting point of these two aspects of elementary koan practice. All of the other koans are either alternative methods or advanced refinements of the exercises and experiences indicated by the first two koans. By putting the first two koans into practice, therefore, it is possible to obtain experiential insight into the keys of all the other koans.

According to Zen teaching, there is really no way to comprehend koans except through themselves. Although the actual experiences of koans open up intellectual understanding, intellectual understanding alone does not open up the actual experiences of koans. As maps, koans show something: Just reading the map is not making the journey, but without reading the map there is no direction. The ordinary mind has no real conception of mental freedom as it is experienced in Zen, so the koan seems impenetrable until we follow its guidance.

In the first koan, the question is posed, "Does a dog have Buddha-nature?" The answer given is "No." The rudimentary exercise of this koan is simply to bring this question and answer to mind from time to time. The exercise is also traditionally performed by just bringing the answer No to mind.

In the second koan, the question is posed, "Are greatly cultivated people still subject to causality?" The answer is given, "They are not blind to causality." The quintessential point of this exercise may also be invoked by simply recollecting, "Not blind to causality."

These basic exercises may be carried on at any time, but it is particularly effective if you take care to call the koan to mind on two specific occasions: whenever you notice you have forgotten about it; and whenever you notice your mind wandering, or seeming to be full of thoughts or feelings. Do this without disrupting accurate awareness of the environment, or of the task at hand.

The very act of bringing up a koan at such times asserts the original freedom and independence of the mind, and thus its attentive practice prevents forgetfulness or preoccupation from monopolizing and controlling the mind. The accompanying acts of recollection and self-monitoring also break the habit of negligence, a self-defeating human weakness that can manifest itself in any form of activity.

The cultivated capacity to assert this power of independence and to bring enhanced attention to bear on any object at will gradually develops into a spontaneous ability to direct attention autonomously. The fortitude of heart this produces cannot be duplicated by fabricated meditation procedures involving self-hypnosis or autosuggestion. When thus empowered, the mind is not obstructed by ordinary affairs, but can manage them with freedom of choice. This happens because the ability to direct and employ the mind deliberately has been built up through persistent exercise of independent will in addition to, not in opposition to, the current of ordinary affairs.

Koans also provide means of focusing the gathered attention on universal principles and objective reality as whole experiences, rather than training the attention on a limited object. Reflecting coherent perceptions within their structures, when correctly understood, koans impart essential meaning and direction to enhanced concentration and awareness.

This meaning and direction depends, naturally, on proceeding to the second stage of basic koan work, linking it to the first. This can again be explained with reference to the first and second koans of this collection as models of the basic genera of exercises of which all other koans represent variations, refinements, combinations, and diagnostic analyses.

The practice of the exercise of No taught in the first koan means bringing No to mind continuously until habitual wandering thought stops and consciousness is calmed and clarified. In Zen Buddhism this is sometimes called realization of nirvana, or emptiness. The practice of the exercise of Not blind to causality taught in the second koan involves observing the processes of events. In technical terms, this is often called arrival at realization of suchness, or being-as-is.

These two aspects of Zen experience have to be integrated to produce wholeness of consciousness. Unless perception of suchness is exercised, the experience of nirvana can deteriorate into quietism instead of the purifying elixir it should be; without nirvanic exercise, perception of reality is hampered by subjectivity and internal chatter. Together these two categories of exercise produce calmness and insight, clarity and precision, wisdom and compassion: Once developed in concert, these qualities then indicate their own unending applications and effects in the life of the individual.

Zen koans are also used for purposes of testing and examining states of mind. Zen teachers use this function of koans to determine students' progress in development of consciousness; Zen students use this function to see teachers and to uncover hidden biases and fixations subconsciously limiting their own minds. Thus koans can help stimulate the process of growth by revealing the limitation of thoughts and ideas based on subjective assumptions.

This use of koans to test mentalities requires a certain degree of Zen psychological knowledge to apply, but parallel examples of its operation can be obtained with familiar materials. A simple method uses the prejudices of the environment, casually providing appropriate stimuli to observe whether an individual or group is infected with the habitual prejudices of the cultural environment, or whether evidence is shown of capacity for independent thought and perception.

In a Western milieu, for example, environmental prejudice is easily elicited by reference to Islam. When people with no knowledge of the Koran or usages of the Prophet are ready to offer opinions on Islam as fact, this represents the working of conditioned bias, not the operation of independent cognition. The inclination to accept unverified opinion simply because of currency or familiarity is a dangerous human weakness that is instrumental in self-deception, and easily exploited for the deception of others. Zen study exposes such fallacies of thought in order to liberate the mind from bondage to the views and attitudes they produce.

The purpose of Zen is to free the mind from the illusion that automatic thinking, the operation of environmentally conditioned prejudices, is real consciousness. Zen does not work in this way, however, when it has itself been subjected to the limitations of biased thinking. Popular Western conceptions of Zen koans as illogical or paradoxical, for example, create an environment of increased susceptibility to confusion and misdirection in those who have imbibed these notions, even subconsciously.

Because the external appearance of Zen symbolism covers an enormous range of imagery, from sublime beauty all the way to violent brutality, it is crucial for the reader to understand that the language of koans is symbolic. Its meanings are not defined by individual items of its surface content, but by the relationships patterned in its underlying structure. Far from being illogical, Zen koans are paragons of logic. This is not always evident to Westerners, however, because the logic of Zen koans is Buddhist logic, which is more experientially oriented than Western philosophy.

Some barriers of environmental prejudice about Zen are extremely tenacious even in Far Eastern cultures, not just in Western cultures. The essential reason for prejudice about Zen, other than misinformation, is simply that its central experience is outside the domain of all acquired conditioning. This ungraspable quality frustrates the compulsion of the ego to identify or associate the self with something, so the threatened ego reacts against its own paranoid conception of the Zen experience.

This psychological resistance to opening up to Zen is quite human and not peculiar to Western people alone. It may appear in any culture, in many different guises:

The gap between the culturally conditioned mind and the liberated Zen mind is such that almost anything from the inventory of habit can be interposed between the inner mind and Zen understanding.

This foible of the human mentality is not brought out into the open by Zen technique in order to criticize and chastise people, but to allow the individual mind to observe directly the mechanism of fixation that holds it back from enlightenment; because it is only by unmasking the inner tyrant that we can ultimately become free.

HOW TO READ THIS BOOK

The text of No Barrier *consists of several tiers of working material. The first tier is a symbolic story or saying of an ancient Zen master. This is followed by a brief comment by Wumen, the later Zen master who compiled these koans in thirteenth-century China. Then there is a final remark by Wumen, this time in verse. The original Chinese text consists of forty-eight of these sets of story, comment, and verse.*

To augment and further illuminate the bare original text, I have also included translations of comments on the same koans by other great masters of Chinese Zen tradition from the eighth to the sixteenth centuries. Some of these are in prose, many are in verse; all of them bring out the inner designs of the koans to make them easier to use.

In a Western cultural milieu where there is no common intimacy with the original Zen ideas or practices, most of the meaning and sense of koans are ordinarily imperceptible, as a matter of natural course. To the translations I have therefore added explanations of the principles and practices, the exercises in perspective and perception, that are indicated in the structure and symbolism of each koan, comment, and verse.

In order to derive maximum benefit from reading this book it must first be understood that Zen texts need to be read several times, in different states of mind, to achieve the degrees of absorption and penetration required to produce the optimum effect. Zen koans are not like ordinary literature and do not yield their enlightenment to emotional or intellectual modes of understanding. A simple program of classical methods for reading this book in a manner consistent with the aims of Zen may be outlined in the following steps:

STEP ONE

Read only the original koans, statements, and verses through, in order. Do not read the translation explanations. Do not try to interpret or remember anything you read. Do not bother making any personal judgments or comparisons.

Note that this manner of reading, far from being the simpleminded mechanical performance it would appear, is itself a fairly difficult Zen exercise in mastery of attention: Therefore it is useful to carry it out with care even if the final purpose and meaning are not immediately evident.

One meaning of this admonition is that it is definitely counterproductive to expect to understand everything at once. Koans are geared to incite feelings of frustration in the arrogant, impatient, possessive part of the psyche, in order to expose the doings of this inner tyrant.

Fortunately, Zen practice provides something much more positive than confusion and worry. As you read the koans and comments, when thoughts occur to you, whether they be random, confused, or insightful, immediately think "No!" and do not pursue them. This is the traditional Zen initiatory exercise of the first koan, which you are now setting in the total design of the whole mandala of koans by viewing them all in this particular manner.

Try to read two koans per day in this way, one in the morning and one at night, calling No to mind as you read the koans, and also from time to time throughout the day. (Note that due to the possibility of distraction or oblivion in those who have not yet mastered attention, this particular exercise is not well suited for beginners when involved in hazardous tasks, such as operating heavy machinery; the second koan is much better in such cases.) At this stage, read the koans in the order they are presented in the book, pairing successive koans in daily readings.

STEP TWO

Now, instead of recalling No! practice focusing attention on the total perception of the immediate present: Take in the whole scene before you at once, again without making any judgments or comparisons, just as if your mind were simply a mirror impartially reflecting whatever comes before it. This is basic concentration on Not blind to causality according to the second koan.

Read through the koans again, as described in the first step, but this time switch the mind to focus on the immediate present whenever you notice thoughts arising. Not blind may be used even in the course of intricate or dangerous tasks, provided you get the proper focus: Make sure you can do it in simple activities before you try it during more complex occupations.

STEP THREE

Returning to the recollection of No! for home base, read through the koans again in the same order and manner, but this time with the explanations. Try to work through all the perceptual shifts and other exercises outlined, immediately remembering No! whenever you lose the thread.

STEP FOUR

Repeat step three, using the recollection of Not blind for home base. Read the koans, comments, verses, and explanations, *using* Not blind *to reorient yourself whenever necessary as you work through the exercises.*

STEP FIVE
Read the book freely now, shifting back and forth between No *and* Not blind *fluidly and accurately according to the emphasis of each koan, to which the foregoing readings are calculated to have sensitized your mind. The purpose of this final step is to cultivate the ability to experience the consciousness of* No *and* Not blind *simultaneously, yet to also be able to shift back and forth at will to focus on either one, according to need: the purifying and awakening function of* No, *or the clarifying and enlightening function of* Not blind.

SUMMARY REMARKS
Three elements are traditionally deemed necessary for successful application of koans to the process of awakening Zen enlightenment: faith, doubt, and resolution.

Faith is needed because the experience of Zen is inconceivable to the ordinary mind and cannot even be imagined until it happens. Therefore faith in the natural possibility of enlightenment is necessary in order to take practical steps toward the unknown.

Doubt is unavoidable because the inconceivable nature of Zen enlightenment necessarily keeps the seeker in a state of suspense, which is of indefinite duration and intensity.

Without the first element of faith, this suspense is humanly unendurable; combined with faith, it enables the individual to question objectively the circumscribed habits of feeling and thought to which he or she tends to return again and again.

According to Zen teaching, the inclination to become engrossed in subjective habits of thought and feeling is precisely what inhibits the human mind from realization of enlightenment. This inclination is so strong that it ordinarily fills any lull, gap, or opening in the continuum of mental habit in an automatic manner. The Zen doubt, buffered with the Zen faith, is a powerful tool for overcoming this limitation of the human mentality; and the Zen koan is an extremely powerful tool for creating and sustaining the Zen doubt.

The final element of resolution is also indispensable, because transcendence of automatic mental habits and consequent freedom and independence of mind are not easy to attain in reality; they require a lifetime of grooming even after awakening to the practical possibility of doing so.

It takes determination simply to recollect Zen koans, let alone carry their mental exercises through; and Zen masters have said that in complete perfect enlightenment there are eighteen major awakenings, and countless minor awakenings. A proverb says, "Those in a hurry do not arrive."

In the final analysis, koans are infinitely rich in existential meaning, but the quality and degree to which their powers to awaken the mind are experienced and lived out depends upon the attention of each individual to his or her own enlightenment.

Zhaozhou's Dog

A monk asked Zhaozhou, "Does even a dog have Buddha-nature?"

Zhaozhou said, "No."

WUMEN SAYS,

To study Zen you must pass through the barrier of the masters; for ineffable enlightenment you need to interrupt your mental circuit. If you do not pass through the barrier of the masters, and do not interrupt your mental circuit, then your consciousness will be attached to objects everywhere.

But tell me, what is the barrier of the masters? This one word No is the unique lock on the door to the source; so it is called the "Barrier of No Locking the Door of Zen."

Those who can pass through the barrier not only see Zhaozhou in person, they will then be able to team up with the Zen masters of all time, and be on a par with them, see with the same eye and hear with the same ear. Would that not be joyous?

Isn't there anyone who wants to pass through the barrier? Arouse a mass of doubt with your whole body, inquiring into this word No, bringing it to mind day and night. Do not understand it as nothingness, do not understand it as the nonexistence of something.

It will be like having swallowed a hot iron pill, which you cannot spit out no matter how hard you try. Washing away your previous misconceptions and misperceptions, eventually it becomes thoroughly familiar. In a natural manner, inside and outside become one; like someone without the power of speech who has had a dream, you can only know it for yourself.

When you suddenly break through, startling the heavens and shaking the earth, it is as though you have obtained a great warrior's sword: meeting Buddhas, you kill the Buddhas; meeting Zen masters, you kill the masters. On the shore of life and death, you attain great independence; in the midst of all sorts of conditions and states of being, you remain perfectly focused even while roaming freely about.

But how do you bring it to mind? Using all of your day-to-day energy, bring up this word No. If you do not allow any gap, you will be like a torch of truth that lights up the moment fire is set to it.

WUMEN'S VERSE

A dog's Buddha-nature
Presents the true directive in full:
As soon as you get into yes and no,
You lose your body and forfeit your life.

ZEN MASTER WUZU'S VERSE

Zhaozhou shows a sword
Whose cold frosty light blazes;
If you go on asking how and what,
It cuts you up into pieces.

2

ZEN MASTER SUSHAN RU'S VERSE
"A dog has no Buddha-nature"—
Kind compassion, deep as the sea.
Those who pursue words and chase sayings
Bury the hearty mind.

TIANTONG RUJING SAID,
When thoughts are flying around your mind in confusion, what do you do? "A dog's Buddha-nature? No." This word No is an iron broom: Where you sweep there is a lot of flying around, and where there is a lot of flying around, you sweep. The more you sweep, the more there is. At the point where it is impossible to sweep, you throw your whole life into sweeping.

Keep your spine straight day and night, and do not let your courage flag. All of a sudden you sweep away the totality of space, and all differentiations are clearly penetrated, so the source and its meanings become evident.

TRANSLATOR'S COMMENTS

Zhaozhou (pronounced Jow-joe) was born in 778 and lived to be one hundred and twenty years old, finally passing away in 897. An exceptionally high-minded master, Zhaozhou was first awakened in the Zen way at the age of eighteen, but he did not open a teaching center until he was eighty years old.

In this koan, the dog represents the state of the unenlightened person, while the Buddha-nature refers both to the essence of enlightenment and the possibility of realizing enlightenment. In this context, enlightenment means full awakening of higher faculties of mind, ordinarily lying dormant beneath subjective preoccupations with thoughts and things.

At the most elementary level, the Zen master's statement that a dog has no Buddha-nature simply draws a distinction between the animal nature and the enlightened nature in humankind. The animal nature is not fully conscious; it reacts to things by instinct and habit, without understanding why. The enlightened nature is the essence of consciousness itself: it sees and understands most directly.

The consciousness of a nonhuman animal is traditionally said to resemble that of the dream consciousness of a human. By a similar analogy, the relationship of ordinary human consciousness to enlightened consciousness is also said to be as that between dreaming and awakening.

The central Zen question is this: What is it that dreams and awakens? The final answer is a realization that can only be found by the individual, in direct experience. The temporary answer is that whatever you may think or imagine this is, that idea or image is a product of mind, not the essence of mind. The significance of this distinction between image and essence is that without direct experiential grounding in the essential nature of consciousness, it is impossible to evaluate the reality of anything that consciousness perceives or conceives.

A concept about consciousness is itself a product of consciousness, not the experience of consciousness in itself. The question in the story at hand can in one sense be paraphrased, "Is it possible to be fully awake while habitual and random thoughts still ramble through the mind?" Here the Zen master says *No*. As we shall see later on, this is not a simple negation, for what the Zen master says in effect is this: In order to see for yourself whether or not it is possible to wake up right in the middle of confusion, first of all stop idle thought and speculation. The *No* is for the questioner, not for the question itself.

Wumen's prose commentary is an attempt to describe a

process of using *No* as an intensive concentration device for clearing the mind and achieving what Buddhists call "stopping" or "cessation." In the full experience of cessation, not only are random thoughts stopped; the whole world view, one's personal idea of reality, is suspended. This is done as an expedient, to free the mind from the limitations of fixed ideas and compulsive habits of thought.

The kind of *No* practice Wumen is talking about was brought to the forefront of popular Zen by the extraordinary master Dahui (pronounced Dah-hway), a couple of generations before Wumen himself. Dahui emphasized this practice in response to the growing complexity of society, because it can help people to cut through mental complications with relative facility.

At the entry level, this exercise is done as follows: Watch what your mind does, and each time you notice "dog" thinking rambling on, bring *No* to mind.

Sound simple? Just try it.

But don't try *too* hard until you have read the rest of this book and learned all about the place of this exercise in the total design of comprehensive Zen Buddhist teaching.

This warning is traditional, because like any tool, it is possible to misuse *No*. You can slip and cut off your head without even knowing it.

A basic form of abuse of *No* is to interpret and practice it in a negative way, using it to make the mind blank and shut out reality instead of using it properly to make the mind clear and open to reality.

This advice is repeated several times in the commentaries of Wumen and the other Zen masters, to which I will now return in order to set *No* into the overall context of Zen practice.

In Wumen's prose commentary, he says, "Do not understand it as nothingness, do not understand it as the absence of something." In practical terms, other Zen masters describe these misunderstandings as the belief that it is necessary to erase all objects from awareness in order to realize the essence of mind and the objective emptiness of subjective projections. In simple terms, neither the practice nor the realization of *No* is a blackout, or a state of consciousness in which no objects are apparent.

Some systems of Buddhist meditation include concentration with no mental object, but this expedient is properly a means of transcending the feeling that our subjective experience of perception corresponds to its objective reality. Thus objectless meditation is only a temporary expedient, and if overused may result in what is known as "intoxication by the wine of absorption," a pathological condition of illusory liberation caused by mental anesthesia.

Wumen's verse comment also repeats this warning by saying that we lose our liveliness if we get into "yes and no." If we get involved in ideas of "yes and no," then "no" becomes negative, the opposite of "yes."

The "true directive" by which Wumen refers to *No* means absolute reality, the ultimate truth, which Buddhists say is beyond thought and ideation: Zhaozhou's *No* means that ultimate reality is not like anything we can imagine; yet that does not mean there is no ultimate reality. If we only follow thoughts coming and going, that is "getting involved in yes and no," frittering away time and energy going back and forth. According to traditional Buddhist yoga, in order to witness absolute reality it is necessary to detach from our conceptual description of reality: that nonattached relationship is neither clinging nor denying, not getting involved in yes and no.

The use of *No* as an instrument is also emphasized in the verse of Zen master Wuzu (pronounced Woo-dzoo), who likens *No* to a sword with which to cut through mental tangles and errant thoughts. Just as Wumen warns against getting involved in "yes and no," Wuzu advises people not to think about *No* conceptually, for that would only lead to fragmentation of mind, not concentration.

The verse of Zen master Sushan (pronounced Soo-shahn) points up the essentially positive intent of the *No* exercise. At the same time, he reiterates the warning against its misapplication, especially through misunderstanding based on superficial literal interpretation.

In the first two lines, Sushan equates *No* with profound compassion, in the sense of release *from* doggishness. The second two lines warn that a literal negative interpretation of *No* does not liberate the mind, but rather inhibits its free functioning. By contrast, therefore, *No* also properly means release *of* the "hearty mind."

One particularly sticky form of doggishness, or the dog-gedness of self-deception, is that of compulsive rationalization. This is in reality one form of superficial literalism, even if it deals primarily with concepts rather than written words per se.

Some people today, for example, understand the question about a dog's Buddha-nature as a metaphysical question about animals. Since Buddhists have always recognized that all living beings are conscious, this question would not arise in a literal sense; it is a purely symbolic representation of a human problem. It is misleading to treat this question as a metaphysical or moral problem; it is simply an immediate alert system within a very direct Zen technique whereby human beings can clear their own mental vision. The commentary of Zen master Tiantong (pronounced Tyen-toong) illustrates this practical function in a manner somewhat similar to that of Wumen.

Some translators do not grant any semantic value to the reply *No*, but render it as if the master in the story had answered with an inarticulate utterance, which they generally say is *Mu*, a Japanese pronunciation of the Chinese *wu*. This reflects a practice of using this meaningless syllable as a kind of mantra or concentration spell to clear the mind of thoughts and detach it from the world of objects.

The original saying was in fact articulate and meaningful,

7

and its original use in meditation was not as a spell. The mental and verbal repetition of *Mu* seems to have been invented in Japan around the year 1900 by an eccentric monk who used it to popularize Zen, which he saw to be on the verge of extinction and in need of emergency measures. Relics of that movement later produced attempts at popularizing "instant" or "jet-age" Zen by throwing people into trances, or driving them to distraction, in highly pressured intensive sessions lasting several days to a week or more at a time.

The general drawbacks of this technique are those of all incantational practices, deriving from the dangers inherent in its effect on unprepared minds. The specific flaw of the *Mu* repetition practice is that it tends to produce a counterfeit experience of emptiness, one that is only an altered state and does not cut through the root of the ego. As the Buddhist giant Nagarjuna wrote, "Emptiness wrongly seen destroys the weak-minded, like a mishandled snake or a misperformed spell."

I have written at length about the first story because of the importance given to it by Wumen and later Zen tradition. In particular, I have reported the traditional warnings of the masters concerning misapplication of this koan because classical lore is full of these caveats, and because such abuse still happens. Today some people still deceive themselves and others by malpractice of this koan, believing themselves to be Zen masters, and trying to teach others to do likewise.

The Wild Fox

Whenever Master Baizhang held a meeting, an old man used to listen to the teaching along with the assembly. When the people of the assembly left, the old man would also leave.

Then one day the old man stayed behind, and the master asked him who he was.

The old man said, "I am not a human being. In the past, in the time of a prehistoric Buddha, I used to live on this mountain. As it happened, a student asked me whether or not greatly cultivated people are also subject to causality. I said that they are not subject to causality, and I fell into the state of a wild fox for five hundred lifetimes. Now I ask you to turn a word in my behalf, so that I may be freed from being a wild fox."

Then the old man asked, "Are greatly cultivated people still subject to causality?"

The master said, "They are not blind to causality."

The old man was greatly enlightened at these words. Bowing, he said, "I have shed the wild fox body, which remains on the other side of the mountain. I am taking the liberty of telling you, and asking you to perform a monk's funeral."

So the master had one of the group hit the sounding

board and announce to the community that they would send off a dead monk after mealtime.

The community debated about this, wondering how it could be so, seeing that everyone was fine and there had been no one in the infirmary.

After the meal, the master led the group to a cave on the other side of the mountain, where he fished out a dead fox with his staff. Then he cremated it.

That evening the master went up in the hall and recounted the foregoing events. Huangbo asked, "An ancient who gave a mistaken answer fell into the state of a wild fox for five hundred lifetimes; what becomes of one who never makes a mistake?"

The master said, "Come here and I'll tell you."

Huangbo then approached and gave the master a slap.

The master clapped and said, "I thought foreigners' beards were red; there is even a red-bearded foreigner here!"

WUMEN SAYS,

If not subject to causality, how could one degenerate into a wild fox? If not blind to causality, how would one be liberated from being a wild fox? If you can set a single eye here, then you will know how the former resident of the mountain gained five hundred lifetimes of elegance.

WUMEN'S VERSE

Not subject, not blind—
Two faces of one die.
Not blind, not subject—
A thousand errors, ten thousand mistakes.

ZEN MASTER GAOFENG MIAO SAID,
The former's "not subject," the latter's "not blind"—is there
*   any gain or loss?*
If there is no causality, how can there be subjection and
*   release?*
If there is, try to come forth and express it clearly.
Is there? Is there?

ZEN MASTER LINGYUAN'S POEM
Clearly saying "not subject," when was the old man ever
*   mistaken?*
Pointedly saying "not blind," how did Baizhang ever
*   understand?*
Nonunderstanding with nonmistaking together express
*   subtle awareness;*
Nonsubjection and nonblindness distinctly represent the
*   true state.*
The causes and effects of the whole potential have reasons:
Rising and sinking in the totality, there is nothing taboo.
"Wrong" is its own wrong; "right" is whose right?
Distracted from the source at the spoken word, one gave
*   rise to deliberation;*
Questioning again, he had it brought up once more.
Secretly watching the rousing of wind and thunder
*   underneath it all,*
With an opposing wind he shouted him around, so the
*   thunder's rumble died.*
Shutting up, the fox returned to his home to hide his
*   disgraceful ineptness;*
Baizhang lifted the autumn moon all the way up over the
*   peak.*

ZEN MASTER BAIZHANG ZHENG'S VERSE

An artist draws a picture of hell,
Depicting hundreds and thousands of scenes.
Setting down his brush, he looks it over,
And feels a shiver run through him.

TRANSLATOR'S COMMENTS

The Zen master Baizhang (pronounced Bye-jong) is supposed to have lived from 720 to 814. He is especially honored for having drafted fundamental guidelines for Zen
communes; thus he is the perfect icon to illustrate a point
about causality, the principle that every act is a cause that
inevitably has a corresponding effect. This principle under-
lies all reason and morality. In Zen schools it is traditionally
stated in terms of a famous saying of Baizhang himself: "A
day without work is a day without food."

In one sense, this koan of the wild fox is aimed directly
at the negative tendencies into which the practitioner may
fall through incorrect or imbalanced practice of the *No*
meditation described in the first story.

According to classical records, one of the most common
negative tendencies is to mistake ignorance (or ignoring)
for transcendence. The first essential point of this wild fox
story, then, is to make it clear that the practice and experience of the Zen Buddhist *No* does not negate causality,
reason, or morality; the real meaning of *No* is to penetrate
the veil of subjective ideas and imaginings that blind us to
objective causal relationships.

Thus Zen practice does not exempt us from what is actually happening; it frees us to see what is really happening.

What Zen exempts us from is the compulsive need to assure ourselves that the world is as we have learned to assume it is. Zen frees us from the mesmerism of wishful and fearful thinking. Emptiness is not nothingness; it is the open door to reality.

The great master Dahui, mentioned in the translator's commentary to the first story, described the effects of mistaken *No* practice as "denying effects of causes and thus becoming crude and careless." A lot of decadent quasi-Zen derives from this form of malpractice.

In the second half of the story, one Huangbo (pronounced Hwong-bwaw) "slapped" the Zen master. Huangbo was a spontaneously enlightened man, but he also apprenticed himself to Zen master Baizhang. This "slap" symbolizes the dismantling of the framework of the teaching event once the point had been made. This is a classical Zen maneuver aimed at inducing the seeker to relinquish attachment to temporary means, such as the didactic story of the old man and the fox in this particular koan.

The phantasmagoric nature of the event in Baizhang's story symbolizes the expedient nature of the teachings. According to a Zen proverb, the student must ultimately transcend the teacher for the transmission of Zen to go through. This proverb also represents transcendence of temporary means, and its message is symbolized in the koan here by the apprentice Huangbo striking the teacher Baizhang.

Recognizing his apprentice's enlightenment, Zen master Baizhang exclaims, "I thought foreigners' beards were red; there is even a red-bearded foreigner here!" In Zen idiom this means, "I know what Zen masters are like; here is another Zen master!" This was Baizhang's recognition of Huangbo's mastery, as illustrated by the apprentice's ability to digest the story of the fox and conclude it in the Zen manner of transcending temporary expedients.

In his prose comment, Wumen says, "If not subject to causality, how could one degenerate into a wild fox?" This rhetorical question is not a philosophical problem; it refers to accurate use of the *No* practice to eliminate the effect of internal talk by stopping its cause. Wumen continues, "If not blind to causality, how would one be liberated from being a wild fox?" This has two meanings. First, it means that in order to be liberated it is necessary to be "blind" in the special sense of not seeing things through the eyes of bondage, or not paying attention to falsehoods and superficialities. Second, it also means that once you are no longer blind to actual reality, you need more than vision; you need cleverness, craft, and wit in the positive senses of these words.

Wumen goes on to say that the ideal integration is not in the position either of the old man or the Zen master; it is in fact up to you: "If you can set a single eye here, you will know how the former resident of the mountain gained five hundred lifetimes of elegance." If bondage and liberation are viewed as ultimately separate from each other, the foxy old man seems to have fallen into bondage because of his attachment to liberation: He would seem to be bound by his very denial of causality. This is a dualistic eye, not a single eye.

In contrast, when it is seen that there is no duality between emptiness and being, the old man would seem to have plunged into bondage as an act of freedom: Freedom became the freedom to take up responsibility, *freely*. In this sense, denying subjection to causality does not mean escapism, but denial of the reality of limitations psychologically imposed by fixation on imagined or fabricated causal chains. This is a single eye, in which freedom of will and responsible involvement are united.

In simple terms, a positive interpretation of the old man's denial of subjection to causality means artful and creative participation in the world, by free will rather than compul-

sion. This is what Wumen refers to as "five hundred lifetimes of elegance."

Wumen concludes, "Not blind, not subject— / A thousand errors, ten thousand mistakes." In colloquial Chinese,
to "meet a mistake with an error" means to make the best
out of a bad situation. Here it means that the ordinary
world is ongoing, and one is not blind to it; and since
nothing is absolutely fixed, there is always potential for
creativity in the very process of change. Thus while nothing in the world is ever perfect, with awareness and autonomy one goes on using imperfect expedients to deal with
imperfect situations.

In the verse of Zen master Gaofeng Miao (pronounced
Gow-fung Myow), the first line denies the presumption that
it is possible to attain real liberation by denying causality,
and the assumption that recognition of causality means loss
of freedom.

The second line further underscores this by recalling the
underlying fact that both subjection and release are predi-
cated on causality, and both obey causal principles.

The third and fourth lines remind us that this is not a
theoretical or philosophical discussion, but a matter of our
actual experience. What are the causes and effects in your
life?

The poem of Zen master Lingyuan (pronounced Ling-
ywen) summarizes and expounds upon these pivotal points
line for line.

"Clearly saying 'not subject,' when was the old man ever
mistaken?" On one level, this means that while it is not
possible to escape causality itself, it is possible to avoid
specific causes. The essential point is to distinguish between the necessary and the possible.

On another level of interpretation, "not subject" stands
for "nonsubjective," which means clear vision. When is that
ever mistaken?

"Pointedly saying 'not blind,' how did Baizhang ever understand?" To say that Baizhang's statement is "pointed" means that Zen attention to causal processes is deliberate, focused, concrete, and practical. To question the possibility of ever understanding refers to the ultimate infinity of reality, and the consequent need for perpetually ongoing awakening. Reality is infinite in both scope and detail, so the development of Zen consciousness in the total sense is a never-ending path.

"Nonunderstanding with nonmistaking together express subtle awareness." "Nonunderstanding" means not making up arbitrary rationalizations; "nonmistaking" means seeing things just as they are. These expressions illustrate awareness more subtle than conceptualization.

"Nonsubjection and nonblindness distinctly represent the true state." "Nonsubjection" here means not being subjective in one's judgments; "nonblindness" means being objective in one's perceptions.

"The causes and effects of the whole potential have reasons." One whose potential is liberated by Zen is able to operate the laws of causality deliberately and intelligently.

"Rising and sinking in the totality, there is nothing taboo." "Rising" means transcendence, "sinking" means return to the world: Those who are fully enlightened are said to be free to come or go, to act in the world or desist, to rise above everything or to get involved in anything. "There is nothing taboo" refers to the completeness of liberation.

" 'Wrong' is its own wrong; 'right' is whose right?" Arbitrarily labeling anything as "wrong" in itself is itself a "wrong" judgment; arbitrarily affirming anything as "right" in itself is a subjective assessment. In order to understand the real meaning and value of such judgments and assessments, it is essential to see them in context and understand the underlying assumptions and premises upon which they are based.

"Distracted from the source at the spoken word, one gave rise to deliberation." This refers to the old man in the story at the time in the remote past when he was questioned by a student about whether or not greatly cultivated people are still subject to causality. The old man was "distracted from the source" by an either/or question, and showed this distraction by an apparently one-sided answer.

"Questioning again, he had it brought up once more." This line refers to the old man bringing up the same question to ask Zen master Baizhang.

"Secretly watching the rousing of wind and thunder underneath it all." This describes the Zen master observing the questioner in order to see what his underlying assumptions are.

"With an opposing wind he shouted him around, so the thunder's rumble died." This is the Zen master's demolition of attachment to a one-sided view of things.

"Shutting up, the fox returned to his home to hide his disgraceful ineptness." The old man stopped doubting and speculating, giving up his conceptual clinging.

"Baizhang lifted the autumn moon all the way up over the peak." Autumn symbolizes the withering and dying of subjective illusions; the moon represents Zen awakening. Baizhang lifted the moon "all the way up over the peak," showing how the ultimate freedom and enlightenment of Zen transcends rigidly divisive either/or thinking in terms of yes and no.

Where did Baizhang lift the moon? Where he liberated the foxy old man? Where he enlightened his students with this story? Where he conceded to his successor Huangbo? All of the above? Try to see both sides of each event, then rise "all the way up over the peak" to a perspective that takes in all views and yet is above them.

One Finger

Whenever Master Judi was questioned, he would just raise a finger. Later a servant boy would also raise a finger when outsiders asked him what the master taught.

When Judi heard of this, he cut off the boy's finger with a knife.

The boy ran out screaming in pain, but Judi called him back. When the boy turned his head, Judi raised a finger. Suddenly the boy attained enlightenment.

When Judi was about to die, he said to a group, "I attained my teacher Tianlong's one-finger Zen, and have used it all my life without exhausting it." So saying, he passed away.

WUMEN SAYS,
The enlightenment of Judi and the boy is not in a finger. If you can see here, then Tianlong, Judi, the boy, and you yourself will be skewered on the same stick.

WUMEN'S VERSE
Judi makes a dunce of old Tianlong;
The sharp blade held up alone tests the little boy.
The great spirit lifted its hands, without much ado,
And split apart the millions of layers of Flower Mountain.

TRANSLATOR'S COMMENTS

Zen master Judi (pronounced Jyw-dee) lived in the ninth century. Little is known about him, except that he was called Judi because he always recited a *dharani*, or meditation spell, by that name. This spell, or concentration formula, is one of those associated with Guanyin (pronounced Gwahn-yin), an essential Buddhist icon representing the activity and efficacy of infinite compassion.

As an otherwise unknown master, Judi is the perfect icon for this koan, because it represents absorption in total unity of being, absorption to the point where there is no longer any subjective feeling or idea of unification itself. At this point, as an earlier Zen master described it, "when you have shed your skin completely, there is only one true reality."

On the primary level of interpretation, therefore, when Zen master Judi would raise a finger, he was simply pointing, both symbolically and directly, to the one true reality that is beyond personal conceptions and judgments. He himself awakened when his Zen teacher Tianlong (pronounced Tyen-loong) simply raised a finger in response to a Zen question.

The story of one finger also carries an important practical teaching. One level of this is signaled by Judi's identification as a devotee of the practice of meditation through the use of a spell. As many people know, the original meaning of "spell" in this sense in English is to render stationary, to fix or train on one point. Thus a spell is a concentration formula repeated to focus the mind steadily. This is analogous to a function of what Indian Buddhists call a *dharani* or a *mantra*.

Some people think that spells are nonsense formulae

whose content has nothing to do with their effect. It is true that there do exist nonsensical formulae, with which it is possible to produce nonsensical concentration. One of the surest signs of a degenerate religious order is belief in mumbo jumbo. Buddhist spells, in contrast, are meaningful to the greatest imaginable degree. This is reflected in Buddhist Chinese, where spells are called "holders of the totality" and "true words."

One of the traditional cautions regarding the use of spells is they can be very dangerous for the inexpert or ill prepared. The danger stems from the fact that repetition of spells can produce absorption so quickly that intense concentration may develop prematurely, without refinement of character or clarification of perception. The result of this imbalance is that personality flaws and subjective biases are actually magnified by concentration, notwithstanding the fact that the practitioner feels fine.

From this perspective, it is easy to see the danger in using "Mu" as a spell. To say that one cannot imagine the perils to which one exposes oneself thereby is nothing but a mathematically precise description of the plight of one "spelled" by a nothing-word. This is one of the best reasons for the ancient doctrine that study of Buddhism after the death of Buddha should ultimately be based on the whole teaching and not a partial teaching.

The sole general exception to the grave cautions and warnings traditionally attached to the use of spells in Buddhism are those spells used to bring to mind the Buddha of Infinite Light and Life. That Buddha represents the reality of universal and cosmic compassion, or objectively real compassion, presiding over a state of being called the Pure Land of Ultimate Bliss. The reason for the exception generally accorded these Pure Land compassion spells is their association with something that is purely benign, an ineffable experience of unconditional mercy and relief.

Nevertheless, the traditional guidelines for successful use of spells do apply to Pure Land spells as well, even if the latter may ordinarily be exempt from the worst perils associated with misuse of spells in general. The benign but relatively ineffective is not as good as the benign and thoroughly effective. The guidelines for genuine efficacy in Buddhist spells are none other than the total design of the whole Buddhist teaching.

This particular koan about one finger makes two essential points about practice, in a typical Zen manner. In the figure of the boy seemingly punished for imitating master Judi is the principle that ignorant imitation, or repetition of superficial forms received at second hand, is not the Way to direct experience of reality. Judi was not imitating his own teacher, who did not raise a finger to every question. Judi had been blasted to kingdom come by his teacher's spontaneous gesture, and spent the rest of his life just pointing to *suchness*. The boy saw Judi raise a finger to every question; had he absorbed the master's message, he would have been able to point to suchness another way, and would not have just mimed the master.

There is another way of looking at this koan. A Zen proverb says that when someone points to the moon, the intention is for others to see the moon, not to have them look at the pointing finger. The purpose of an exercise, such as reciting a spell or raising a finger to see how people understand, is solely to obtain the effect, not to become a slavish devotee of that particular exercise. From this perspective, "cutting off" the boy's finger is not punishment; it symbolizes graduation.

In the graphic terminology of Taoist spiritual alchemy, an ancient cousin of Zen, when the peak effect of an exercise is obtained, it is necessary to "remove the fire" from under the "elixir" to prevent the medicinal ingredients in the elixir from getting "stale." Buddhist scriptures and Zen teachings also speak figuratively of discontinuing the medicine once the sickness is cured, lest "the medicine itself cause an illness."

In the relatively simple methodology of some of the ancient Zen schools, the cutting off of an observance in which one has become totally absorbed could be something of a shock, as represented here by the screaming boy. But now the teacher calls attention to the effect of the teaching, attention that had hitherto been focused on the teaching as a cause. The sudden shift from absorption in practice to absorption in realization is represented as the boy suddenly attaining enlightenment.

Wumen's prose comment starts out by saying in effect that the pointing finger is not the moon, the signpost is not the destination. Then he invites us to see the moon of reality ourselves, to which all the players in this koan are pointing. He says we are all "skewered on the same stick," showing us ourselves in the context of the totality of everything.

In his verse, Wumen begins by saying that Judi makes a dunce of Tianlong. This alludes to his deathbed remark that he got his "one-finger Zen" from Tianlong. Wumen reminds us not to take this kind of talk literally to mean the transmission of a certain form or habit, and to remember that real Zen masters do not deal in secondhand realizations.

The second line of Wumen's verse speaks of the "sharp blade" of Judi "testing" the boy; this represents penetrating insight into absolute reality admitting of no comparison or likeness, making us shed the habit of fixating on secondary things as if they were ultimately real.

The last two lines of Wumen's verse allude to an ancient Chinese legend about a giant spirit splitting a huge mountain. This is simply used as a colorful metaphor describing what Zen Buddhists call "direct pointing" employed as a means of cutting through a mass of random imaginings. By his actions, Judi first cut through a mountain of subjective

22

thoughts and concepts, then shattered the monolithic perspective of oneness.

In this way, unity and differentiation are both one and yet distinct: The particulars of the many are all part of one whole, the one whole is comprised of the many. This koan focuses on unity; differentiation is eclipsed, except for the obvious warning that undifferentiated unity is an illusion produced by freezing the mind.

The whole koan may be summed up with a verse on this koan by the great Zen master Yuanwu (pronounced Ywenwoo). This humorous verse summarizes the points raised by the koan, and also reminds us to see Judi's way of teaching in its proper context and not to imitate it blindly:

How could it be easy to reply
To the causal conditions of question and answer?
It's hard to be really stylish if you have no money.
There's something in his heart, but he cannot say it;
In his hurry he just holds up a finger.

"How could it be easy to reply / To the causal conditions of question and answer?" Here Yuanwu takes up the position of pleading Judi's case, saying it cannot be easy to give an answer; the intricacy and scope of total reality are ultimately infinite. No one can encompass the whole truth in words. This is why Judi simply sums everything up in one.

"It's hard to be really stylish if you have no money." Playfully chiding Judi for being simplistic and crude, in reality Yuanwu is repeating the traditional Buddhist teaching that complete enlightenment includes skill in devising means of helping and liberating others, here represented by "money."

"There's something in his heart"—Judi was undeniably enlightened in the sense of his realization of the ultimate truth—"but he cannot say it"—ultimate reality cannot, by its very nature, be expressed in words; so "in his hurry he just holds up a finger"—his simplicity is not a reduction, but an affirmation of the infinity of reality and the teachings it contains.

A popular Zen meditation theme says, "All things return to One; where does the One return?" This is the way to work on the koan of Judi's finger.

The Foreigner Has No Whiskers

Huo-an said, "Why has the Foreigner from the West no whiskers?"

WUMEN SAYS,
Study must be genuine study, enlightenment must be real enlightenment. This foreigner must be seen in person before you understand; but when you talk about a personal meeting, there's already a dichotomy.

WUMEN'S VERSE
In the presence of an ignoramus,
Do not talk about a dream.
The foreigner having no whiskers
Adds obscurity to awareness.

TRANSLATOR'S COMMENTS

"The Foreigner from the West" refers to the Indian Buddhist master Bodhidharma, who is regarded as the founder of Zen in China. He is traditionally depicted as having a heavy beard.

Zen master Huo-an (pronounced Hwaw-ahn) lived in the late twelfth century, near the time of Wumen himself. Huo-an was a high-minded individual who did his utmost to avoid notoriety. Very little is known of this master other than a few stories and poems attributed to him.

In this koan, Huo-an asks why the bearded founder of Zen has no beard. Like other koans, this is not an illogical, whimsical bit of word play, but a symbolic reminder of an aspect of reality.

The figure of the Zen founder is ordinarily used to represent the real self or the essential mind, as understood in Zen experience. This self is called a Foreigner because it is unfamiliar to the culturally conditioned mind. To say that the Foreigner has no beard is to say that the real self or essential mind is not identical to the superficial aspects of personality or outward appearance.

In his prose comments, Wumen underscores the importance of setting aside superficial appearances to get at realities when he says that it is necessary to study reality by means of reality itself. He goes on to highlight the need for direct personal experience rather than secondhand theory; "this foreigner must be seen in person before you understand."

Wumen's prose remarks conclude with a reminder that the Zen founder is none other than one's real self, which has been there all along: "When you talk about a personal meeting, there's already a dichotomy." This means that Zen awakening does not come through trying to assimilate to an image, but through spontaneous realization of the fundamental essence of awareness underlying all appearances.

In his verse comment, Wumen aims the thrust of this koan at the use of the koan itself, warning the onlooker not to approach it through its superficial appearance. The question in the koan is deliberately contrived to elicit a certain way of seeing; but to someone who sees only the obvious conundrum, the outward form of the koan causes confusion.

This is one of many examples where Wumen's comments mainly serve to set up a signpost pointing out a pitfall for the unwary.

Up in a Tree

Master Xiangyan said, "Suppose someone is up in a tree, holding on to a branch by his teeth, his hands without a grip on a limb, his feet without a toehold on the trunk. Someone under the tree asks about the meaning of Zen. If he does not answer, he is avoiding the question; but if he does answer, he loses his life. At just such a time, how would you reply?"

WUMEN SAYS,

No matter how eloquent you are, it is of no use at all; even if you can explain the whole Canon, it is still of no avail. If you can give an answer here, you will bring to life your previous road of death, and kill your previous road of life. Otherwise, if not, just wait for the future, to ask the Buddha Maitreya.

WUMEN'S VERSE

Xiangyan is truly inept;
His vile poison is limitless.
He silences Zen students' mouths,
So demon eyes squirt out from all over their bodies.

ZEN MASTER BAIYAN SAID,
Xiangyan made the whole earth into a glowing furnace, its fierce flames reaching through the sky: even iron and steel melt at once.

ZEN MASTER FENYANG'S VERSE
Xiangyan grips the tree with his teeth, showing many people:
He wants to lead his peers to the fundamental reality.
Try to deliberate, and you are grasping from words;
Countless are those who have lost their lives.
I will open a way through the confusion for you:
When the clouds have dispersed in the eternal sky, sun and moon are new.

ZEN MASTER YUELIN'S VERSE
Xiangyan climbs a tree—
Stop, stop, stop, stop!
If you try to ask about—
Complications and clichés.

TRANSLATOR'S COMMENTS

Zen master Xiangyan (pronounced Shyahng-yen) lived in the ninth century. He was especially noted for his unusual poetry. In Zen lore, Xiangyan is represented as having formerly been an intellectual who failed to realize the essence of mind because of his preoccupation with intellectual exercise. Frustrated by this failure, he eventually gave up his studies and secluded himself to meditate on the original mind. Then one day he suddenly awakened to the truth of

Zen when he heard the sound of pebbles striking a clump of bamboo.

Like the previous one, this koan takes the form of a question deliberately constructed to elicit a specific insight. The image of the man holding onto a tree branch with his teeth symbolizes the attachment of a conditioned mind to the fragment of reality perceptible through the worldview to which the mind is habituated by personal and cultural history. Xiangyan himself was quite familiar with this state, having spent so many years in trying to grasp Zen through intellectual exercise.

In order to realize Zen enlightenment, it is necessary to be able to stand apart from the worldview or mind-set to which one has been conditioned, yet without warping the mind's capacity for constructive organization. Thus Xiangyan's man in the tree has to let go of his precarious grip with his teeth in order to "answer a question about Zen," meaning that he must give up his intellectual fixations to realize Zen; yet he must not allow this detachment to make him an ineffective escapist and thus "lose his life."

Wumen's prose comments begin by stressing the point that this koan is not a riddle to be solved by intellectual exercise. He goes on to say that proper work with the koan will "bring to life your previous road of death," meaning that it will awaken hitherto dormant insight; and it will "kill your previous road of life," meaning that it will free you from compulsive habits of thought.

Wumen concludes his prose remarks by reminding us not to get tangled up in the facade of the koan itself. If you cannot find the answer, he says, "wait for the future, to ask the Buddha Maitreya." Maitreya is the name of the mythological Buddha of the Future, who is to come at the end of the present eon to rescue those as yet unable to attain enlightenment. Thus Wumen says in effect that it is necessary to be infinitely patient and wait out confusion, rather than exacerbate it by tangling with this koan on a merely intellectual level.

Wumen begins his verse commentary by calling Xiangyan "truly inept." This means that he has attained true Zen "ineptness," which is a humorous way of representing transcendence of the "cleverness" of idle intellectualism.

Wumen then qualifies his statement by saying that Xiangyan's "vile poison is limitless." Zen teaching is often called "vile" and "poisonous" in that it drives off delusions and "kills" false thinking. Xiangyan's "poison" is "limitless" in that his device does not accommodate any subjective ideas or admit of any theoretical solutions.

In the last two lines of his verse, Wumen summarizes the intended effect of Xiangyan's device in very colorful terms. He "silences" the "mouths" (quiets the talking minds) of Zen seekers, so that "demon eyes squirt out all over their bodies" —intellectual fixations and arbitrary ideas fall away from the purified consciousness, having no inherent reality to sustain them without the support of compulsive habits of thought.

The comment of Zen master Baiyan (pronounced Byeyen) graphically illustrates this functional aspect of Xiangyan's device. The image of the "glowing furnace" is a classical Zen symbol of a state of mind so focused on the ineffable that no random thought or imagination can linger. Idle thoughts become like snowflakes falling onto a blazing fire, evaporating at once. Baiyan extends this metaphor to the greatest degree of intensity, saying that "even iron and steel melt at once," to illustrate the potency of Xiangyan's device as a tool for stilling the wandering mind.

The verse of Zen master Fenyang (pronounced Funyahng) makes it clear that the point of Xiangyan's device is not in the surface expression. He says that the point is in stopping subjective thinking in order to let reality become apparent of itself; therefore he cautions the onlooker not to grasp for the meaning from the words, for that would lead to a dead end.

Fenyang concludes by describing the actual experience of resolution of this koan, which is by nature inconceivable and ineffable; it cannot be expressed directly, so poetic imagery and symbolism are used to allude to the experience. The "clouds" represent delusions, the "eternal sky" represents the true mind; the "sun and moon" stand for knowledge of absolute and relative realities, being "new" stands for immediacy and spontaneity. When the mind is freed of delusions, rational and intuitive cognition both attain more intimate relationship with objective reality.

Finally, the verse of Zen master Yuelin (pronounced Yweh-lin) highlights the contrived character of the setup of the koan and reminds us not to get enmeshed in the external appearance, and not to go on thinking about it conceptually. The second line, "Stop, stop, stop, stop!" is both a warning not to pursue thoughts and a signpost saying that at bottom "stopping" the wandering mind is what this koan is all about. As Yuelin concludes, if you don't "stop," but go on posing the question as an intellectual conundrum, all you will come up with are "complications and clichés."

6

Buddha Picks up a Flower

In ancient times, at the assembly on Spiritual Mountain, Buddha picked up a flower and showed it to the crowd.

Everyone was silent, except for the saint Kashyapa, who broke out in a smile.

Buddha said, "I have the treasury of the eye of truth, the ineffable mind of nirvana, the most subtle of teachings on the formlessness of the form of reality. It is not defined in words, but is specially transmitted outside of doctrine. I entrust it to Kashyapa the Elder."

WUMEN SAYS,
Gautama Buddha acted shamelessly; he pressed the free into slavery. Hanging out mutton, he sold dog meat, as if it were so wonderful.

Suppose everyone had smiled at that moment? How could the treasury of the eye of truth be transmitted? And if Kashyapa had not smiled, how could the treasury of the eye of truth be transmitted?

If you say there is any transmitting the treasury of the eye of truth, Buddha is fooling villagers; if you say there is no transmitting it, why does he only approve of Kashyapa?

WUMEN'S VERSE

When he picked up the flower,
The tail was already showing;
Kashyapa broke into a smile,
People and spirits were at a loss.

ZEN MASTER SONGXIAN SAID,

One's garbled words disturb the crowd, another took up the
empty and accepted the false. Both of them were seeing ghosts
in front of their skulls. Too bad none of them at the meeting
were robust; as a result the chase still goes on.

ZEN MASTER SONGHUA SAID,

When Buddha held up the flower, he was "so concerned for
his children that he was unconscious of being unseemly."
When Kashyapa smiled, he "stuck his brains in a bowl of
glue."

TRANSLATOR'S COMMENTS

Spiritual Mountain is a place where Buddha taught on certain occasions. It is also called Vulture Peak. According to Buddhist lore, this is where a hitherto unknown dispensation in Buddhism called the *Lotus Scripture* was revealed for the first time in the present eon; and it is the site of a fundamental schism between universal and sectarian Buddhists, which legend says took place on the very occasion, and for the very reason, of the revelation of the *Lotus Scripture* by the Buddha. This koan is a recapitulation of that monumental event, performed in the austere style of the

Linji school of Zen Buddhism, to which master Wumen and most of the other commentators in this volume belonged.

The *Lotus Scripture*, and this Zen koan, are about what Indian Buddhists call *tathatā*, which means "thusness" or "suchness," meaning the way things are in objective reality, without subjective distortion. This experience of reality is also called *yathābhūta*, which means "being-as-is," reality as it is perceived after the mind is freed from the limitations of its own conceptual attachments.

In practical terms, the scripture and the story are about realization of what Buddhists call the identity of samsara and nirvana. Samsara means routine existence, birth and death, the arising and passing away of thoughts and feelings; in very general terms, samsara means the world and all that it is and all that goes on in it. Nirvana literally means extinction, in reference to the stilling of compulsive behavior, including compulsive thought, and the attainment of complete peace of mind.

Realization of the unity of samsara and nirvana is a critical issue in Buddhism, one of those in which the greatest hopes are reposed at the very same time that the gravest warnings are posted around it.

The good news is that the union of samsara and nirvana is accessible, in the direct experience of suchness. The bad news is that an immature understanding of the principle leads right back into a quagmire of attachment to thoughts and things, although now with the empty grace of imagining this state to be none other than ultimate reality.

The essential point of traditional warnings is that when people who are too hasty and greedy for their own good hear that samsara and nirvana are one, they decide they can choose to keep samsara just as it is and claim to have attained nirvana to boot. The practical fact of the matter is, however, that it is necessary to realize nirvana before you can understand what it actually means to say that nirvana and samsara are not separate. Only after you have cleared your mind can you see that nothing has in itself any power to confuse you; before that it is only theory and talk.

For this reason, it is said that the teachings on the unity of samsara and nirvana are elixir for those who can digest them, poison for those who cannot digest them.

The comments of Wumen and the other Zen masters are all about warding off such problems with the practice of this view. One basic problem is the temptation to identify suchness with what is perceived as ordinary reality by the conventionally conditioned mind; another is the temptation to remain absorbed either in specific manifestations of suchness (like natural scenery) or in the ineffable totality of suchness, and thus to stay at a low level of effective realization by excessive stilling of mind or fixation on a specific instance of realization. A Zen proverb says, "This is It, but as soon as you recognize it explicitly, then it's not It anymore."

When Wumen says in his prose comment that Buddha "acted shamelessly," he means that the Buddha pointed to the absolute aspect of suchness, in which all discriminatory thought is inapplicable and everything is essentially equal. To say that he "pressed the free into slavery" means that he indicated the identity of nirvana ("freedom") and samsara ("slavery"). In the total context of Buddhism revealed in the *Lotus Scripture*, nirvana is not the final goal but rather a means to open the mind to the infinity of reality.

Wumen adds that Buddha "hung out mutton but sold dog meat," an old expression for what we call "bait and switch" tactics. Buddha originally spoke of nirvana as ultimate peace to induce people to leave their vexing and harrying mundane preoccupations aside; only after they had done this were they given to realize that this nirvana was just an expedient, designed to liberate them from the confines of subjective imagination to the infinity of the real world outside.

Wumen goes on to question us about how to distinguish

between real and false understanding of the identity of samsara and nirvana in the experience of suchness. In order to answer these questions we have to examine our experience and distinguish between subjective assumptions and objective perceptions.

Finally Wumen concludes his prose remarks with a traditional Zen statement on transmission of this subtle teaching. In one sense there is no transmission of any direct knowledge or understanding from one person to another, because the teaching is reality itself and the direct knowledge and understanding of suchness must be firsthand. In another sense there is transmission, in that conscious participation in reality is not a subjective experience, but is by nature shared in common with anyone who has the same objective experience. Kashyapa was already enlightened when he met Buddha; he recognized Buddha's enlightenment, and Buddha recognized his enlightenment.

The comments of Zen master Songxian (pronounced Soong-shyen) combine description and warning in traditional Zen double-entendre style.

"One's garbled words" refers to Buddha's symbolic identification of samsara and nirvana in the experience of suchness by the act of raising the flower and associating this direct perception with the heart of nirvana. Buddha's words "disturb the crowd" in two senses. First, by speaking of unification his statement supposes separation; second, by speaking of unity his statement leaves room for misconception of subjective perceptions as objective truth.

Songxian continues, "another took up the empty and accepted the false." This refers to Kashyapa's integrated understanding of absolute reality ("the empty") and relative reality ("the false"). By appearing to chide Kashyapa, Songxian also warns people not to misinterpret; his final remark castigating the crowd indicates that everyone must personally have the direct experience of the "flower" of reality in order to understand.

The comments of Zen master Songhua (pronounced Soong-hwah) are also covert warnings about misunderstanding, couched in terms of reproof. To be "so concerned for your children that you are unconscious of being unseemly" refers to the way a Buddha or Zen master bends over backward to set up devices to communicate the ineffable; the intention is not to get stuck on the appearance, just to get the point. To "stick your brains in a bowl of glue" means to remain fixed in a static realization; the point is to keep the mind open to the infinity of reality, not to congratulate yourself at having found the nose on your face.

7

Wash Your Bowl

A monk asked Zhaozhou, "I have just joined the community, and I request the teacher's instruction."

Zhaozhou inquired, "Have you had your breakfast gruel yet?"

The monk said, "I have had my gruel."

Zhaozhou said, "Then go wash your bowl."

That monk had an insight.

WUMEN SAYS,

When Zhaozhou opens his mouth you see his guts, as he reveals his heart. If this monk didn't listen truly, he'd call a bell a pitcher.

WUMEN'S VERSE

Just because it is so distinctly clear,
That makes attainment slow.
If he had known the lamp was fire,
The rice would have been cooked long ago.

ZEN MASTER NANTANG'S VERSE

Zhaozhou points out "Wash your bowl"—
Zen seekers who scramble and race waste effort madly:
They don't even know where to look for everyday affairs;
They are clearly told, but are as blind and deaf.

ZEN MASTER HUGUO'S VERSE

Finding out the principles of things makes up the livelihood
of the house;
When you're able to meet the opportunity of the time, then
you know the heart.
Let us give thanks to the impartiality of the spring wind;
The peaches and plums of the poor houses also create
shade.

TRANSLATOR'S COMMENTS

This is the same Zhaozhou as in the first koan. This story, like the preceding one, can be read as a symbolic demonstration pointing to direct experience of immediate reality without conceptual adornment, the initiatory experience of Zen.

Furthermore, when "breakfast" is understood metaphorically to mean this very experience itself, the story also points to the next step, of transcending the subjective register of initial realization so as to "clean the vessel" for yet further enlightenment.

Wumen's prose comment begins by acknowledging Zhaozhou's demonstration of "suchness" as an illustration of the broadest common denominator of Buddhist experience. He concludes by warning us not to let the unifying perspective of suchness blur authentic distinctions within the totality.

Wumen's verse on this koan is one of my very favorites. Zen masters often chide seekers for searching in recondite places for truths that can be seen near at hand in everyday life. The verse of Zen master Nantang (pronounced Nahntahng) also underscores this point, in an even more explicit manner.

The verse of Zen master Huguo (pronounced Hoogwaw) begins by returning to the matter of "not mistaking a bell for a pitcher," or clarifying knowledge of differentiation within the total unity of suchness. The last two lines refer to the living meaning of suchness itself, describing it as the "impartiality of the spring wind," and speak thereby of the effectiveness and meaningfulness of things just as they are, the "peaches and plums of the poor houses," unadorned by grandiose illusions.

8

The Wheelmaker

Master Yue-an asked a seeker, "The original wheel-maker made wheels with a hundred spokes. If you take away both sides and remove the axle, what does this clarify?"

WUMEN SAYS,
If you can understand directly, your eyes will be like a shooting star, your mind like a flash of lightning.

WUMEN'S VERSE
Where the wheel of potential turns,
Even experts are bewildered:
All around the compass, zenith and nadir,
South, north, east, west.

TRANSLATOR'S COMMENTS

Yue-an (pronounced Yweh-ahn) was a later Zen master who flourished not long before the time of Wumen himself. He is historically obscure, and no other Zen masters besides Wumen and Wumen's teacher Yuelin wrote verses on this Zen koan constructed by Yue-an.

In the koan, the wheels of a hundred spokes represent the conceptual structures we use to explain the world in everyday life. The axle is the basic mind. The wheels move, the axle does not; but the wheels cannot move without the axle.

The mental exercise of dismantling structures, taking the "wheels" off the "axle," is not a destruction or rejection of rationality, as some Zen popularizers have claimed; it is a means of getting to the source of mental construction, the basic mind itself. Accordingly, another classical version of this story has the Zen master conclude by drawing an empty circle—the traditional Zen symbol for the basic mind in its pristine innocence—and saying, "Don't stick to the zero point of the scale." Not "sticking to the zero point of the scale" means realizing not only essence but also function; it is the unification of nirvana and samsara.

This koan is all in the doing, not the discussing, so Wumen's comments are extremely brief. In his prose remarks he says that if you understand this koan *directly*, then "your eyes will be like a shooting star, your mind like a flash of lightning." These images of light and speed allude to the instantaneous understanding of the special knowledge Buddhists call *prajna*, which is direct insight into the essence of things.

Wumen also begins his verse by affirming that *prajna* is

not ordinary conceptual knowledge: "Where the wheel of potential turns," he says, referring to the activation of the dormant faculty of direct understanding, "even experts are bewildered." The image of the "expert" symbolizes the conceptual mind that thinks it knows everything through its ideas. Perceiving immediate reality as it is in the process of becoming is an experience that by its very nature baffles the conceptual process, which is inherently retrospective in that it functions by selecting and assembling recollections, not by dealing directly with *suchness*. When you experience the world in the immediacy of present becoming through the opened eye of Zen, everything is fresh and new, everything is unique and unimagined. In his final lines, Wumen simply gasps in awe as he observes the light of this enlightenment pervading everywhere.

As I mentioned before, very little can be profitably said about this koan, and most of the later masters are silent about it. There is a verse by Wumen's teacher Yuelin, however, that encapsulates the whole matter:

The ocean god knows it's valuable, but doesn't know its
  price;
Left in the human world, its light illumines the night.
The founder of Zen smiles and nods his head;
Who knows the action hasn't a seam or gap?

The "ocean god" symbolizes oceanic consciousness, which is like the all-encompassing light of immediate awareness engulfing everything. The "value" of this koan is in its effect; the "price" is its outward form: To know the value but not the price means to get the real point of the koan and not be concerned with its superficial appearance.

What is "left in the human world" is the potential for this Zen awakening, and tools like this koan for fostering and reflecting Zen awakening. The "light" of the enhanced awareness released by this exercise "illumines" the "night" of ignorance, bringing the joyful recognition of the basic mind, which is the real "founder of Zen." In this realization there is no room for doubt or speculation, so there isn't "a seam or gap," and since you are one with the realization itself, "who knows?"

9

The Buddha Capable of Great Penetrating Knowledge

A monk asked Master Rang of Xingyang, "The Buddha Capable of Great Penetrating Knowledge sat on the site of enlightenment for ten eons, but the realities of enlightenment did not become apparent to him, and he was unable to fulfill the way of Buddhahood. Why was that?"

The master said, "Your question is quite clearly to the point."

The monk said, "Since he was sitting on the site of enlightenment, why was he unable to fulfill the way of Buddhahood?"

The master said, "Because he did not fulfill Buddhahood."

WUMEN SAYS,

I only admit the old barbarian knows; I don't admit the old barbarian understands. If ordinary people know, they are sages; if sages understand, they are ordinary people.

WUMEN'S VERSE

How is mastering the body as good as mastering the mind?
When you have mastered mind, the body is no worry.
If body and mind are both perfectly mastered,
Why should spiritual immortals also be entitled as lords?

GUSHAN'S VERSE

Planting grain does not produce beans;
Can boiling sand make a meal of rice?
The Buddha Capable of Great Penetrating Knowledge
Only saw one side of things.

TRANSLATOR'S COMMENTS

Master Rang (pronounced Zrahng) of Xingyang (pronounced Shing-yahng) is a shadowy figure of the ninth to tenth century, one of the masters of the high-minded Gui-Yang school (pronounced Gway-Yahng).

This koan refers to a story in the famous *Lotus Scripture*, which has already been mentioned in my comments on the sixth koan, "Buddha Picks Up a Flower." In this popular story, a prehistoric Buddha sat perfectly still for ten eons, but did not yet awaken to Buddhahood. Only after having sat through further eons of "showers" of heavenly rain did that Buddha actually realize Buddhahood.

The lesson taught in the scripture is to go beyond the quiescence of nirvana, realizing that the peace of nirvana is just a means of gaining access to the infinite endlessness of continuous awakening to reality.

In his comments, Wumen says, "I only admit the old barbarian knows; I don't admit the old barbarian understands." The "old barbarian" stands for the ancient Buddha in the story, who at this point only had "knowledge," which here means the heart of nirvana, or the peace of the absolute, but lacked "understanding," which here means knowledge of differentiations of samsara, or the relative world.

Wumen goes on to explain, "If ordinary people know, they are sages." The penetrating insight of this special knowledge lifts the mind beyond ordinary habit-ridden conditioned consciousness. But that is not the end: "If sages understand," Wumen continues, "they are ordinary people." After Buddhists attain the penetrating insight of nirvana, then they can return freely to the ordinary world of relative reality, "not blind to causality."

In Wumen's verse comment, he says, "How is mastering the body as good as mastering the mind?" The Buddha in the story sat still in meditation for ten eons, yet still did not awaken; so Wumen says that realization of essence (mind) is better than mastery of form (body). When both mind and body are mastered, he adds, the completely enlightened individual ("spiritual immortal"), being independent and autonomous, has no need of worldly distinction ("be entitled as a lord").

The simple but charming little verse on this koan by Zen master Gushan (pronounced Goo-shahn) sums up the point very neatly. When he says that grain does not produce beans and sand does not turn into rice, Gushan invokes a traditional Zen symbol for the objective laws of causality. In his state of absolute stillness, the ancient Buddha "only saw one side of things"—in the words of the second koan in this collection, he may have been "not subject," but he was not as yet "not blind."

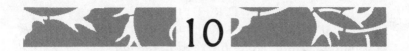

10

Alone and Poor

A monk named Qingshui said to Caoshan, "Qingshui is alone and poor—please help out."

Caoshan said, "Reverend Qingshui!"

Qingshui said, "Yes?"

Caoshan said, "You have already drunk three cups of the wine of the purists of Zen, yet you still say you haven't wet your lips."

WUMEN SAYS,

Qingshui passed up the opportunity; what was going on in his mind?

Caoshan had eyes; he profoundly discerned the states of those who came to him.

Even so, tell me, where did Qingshui drink wine?

WUMEN'S VERSE

Poor as the poorest,
Brave as the bravest,
Though he had nothing to live on,
He dared to joust with the rich.

ZEN MASTER FOYIN'S VERSE

Qingshui alone and poor—his mind's too coarse:
Caoshan takes him along the road to the inn.
Three cups of the purists' lip-wetting wine;
Add a cup after intoxication, and all seems naught.

ZEN MASTER HUANSHAN'S VERSE

Caoshan, used to using the Zen purists' wine,
Pours it out entirely in front of others.
The intoxication topples Zen seekers all over the world;
Yet Your Reverence is still not aware.

TRANSLATOR'S COMMENTS

Qingshui (pronounced Ching-shway) was a disciple of Zen master Caoshan (pronounced Tsao-shahn). Caoshan was one of the greatest Zen teachers of the ninth century. He was one of the first masters to analyze koans explicitly and systematize them according to their inner structures.

When Qingshui says he is alone and poor, this means he has attained nirvana: "alone" symbolizes independence, "poverty" symbolizes freedom from attachments. He approaches a complete Zen master because he knows this is not yet ultimate enlightenment.

In response, Caoshan calls to the seeker. What the Zen master is really doing here is calling to Life as it expresses itself through this individual. When the seeker spontaneously responds, "Yes?" Caoshan tells him that *there* he has his answer.

When the Zen master chides his student for "claiming his lips were not even wet" in spite of having drunk "three cups" of the "wine of Zen," he is addressing us, as usual. To cling to the peace of individual nirvana, or "not being subject to causality," as if it were the ultimate goal, is equivalent to ignoring the unity and infinity of Life. This is represented by "claiming his lips are not even wet." The "three cups of wine," in contrast, represent complete realization of the absolute truth (nirvana), the relative world (samsara), and the way to realize their union (what Buddhists call the Middle Way). Caoshan indicates that these three realizations are inherent in the essence of mind even when it is in a nirvanic state; all that is necessary is to awaken the function in response to potential.

Wumen begins his prose comments by saying that Qingshui "passed up the opportunity," which is a classical Zen image for being stuck on nirvana and failing to come to life anymore. Wumen then goes on to praise Caoshan for his precise discernment of this state. This exact discernment of the conditions of others is an essential prerequisite for Zen teachers.

Wumen concludes his prose comments by asking us where Qingshui drank wine. "Qingshui" stands for the seeker of truth: Where is that response in us? What mind says "Yes?"

Wumen's verse comment reiterates the image of poverty, then adds the idea of bravery. According to the *Flower Ornament Scripture*, the primary text of all Buddhism, when you transcend attachment to your ego, then you become fearless. This is Qingshui reaching forward for infinite life after absolute nirvana, approaching the source of the teaching with a completely open mind. Wumen concludes, in praise of Qingshui, "Though he had nothing to live on"—he was purely nirvanic and lacked skill in handling samsara—"He dared to joust with the rich": His nirvana was so deep he could understand the rest of the truth in one encounter with a complete master.

The verse of Zen master Foyin (pronounced Fwaw-yin)

also describes the relative simplicity of sheer nirvana, and how a complete Zen master takes people back to the source of both nirvana and samsara. At the conclusion of his verse, Foyin acknowledges that Qingshui was really enlightened, as Caoshan said; he is simply representing a new illuminate who has yet to realize that after complete enlightenment, enlightenment is nothing out of the ordinary.

The verse of Zen master Huanshan (pronounced Hwahn-shahn) praises the mastery of Caoshan in being able to express *suchness,* and to induce *suchness* to express itself consciously through another individual, with the simplest of devices.

The third line reminds us that the Buddha-nature, the essence of mind to which Caoshan calls, is inherently present in everyone.

The last line warns us not to act like Qingshui ("Your Reverence") pretends, clinging to a negative and solitary nirvana. As an ancient Zen proverb says, "Buddha does not remain in Buddhahood: This is called the real field of blessings."

Testing Hermits

Zhaozhou went to where a hermit was staying and asked, "Is there? Is there?"

The hermit held up a fist.

Zhaozhou said, "A ship cannot moor where the water is shallow." Then he left.

Zhaozhou also went to where another hermit was staying and asked, "Is there? Is there?"

That hermit also raised a fist.

Zhaozhou said, "Can concede, can deny, can kill, can enliven." Then he bowed.

WUMEN SAYS,

Both alike raised a fist: Why did he agree with one and not the other? Where is the riddle? If you can utter a pivotal word here, you will see that Zhaozhou's tongue has no bone; he helps up and knocks down with great freedom.

But even so, Zhaozhou was nevertheless exposed by the two recluses: If you say that either of the recluses was better or worse, you still lack the eye for Zen learning; but if you say neither was better or worse, you also still lack the eye for Zen learning.

WUMEN'S VERSE

Eyes like shooting stars,
Mind like flashing lightning;
The sword that kills,
The sword that gives life.

ZEN MASTER YUN-AN SAID,

"A ship cannot moor where the water is shallow"—*there are echoes in the words.* "Can concede, can deny," *and a bow—there are barbs concealed in the statement. Old Zhaozhou may be said to have used all of his magical powers; the recluses were skillfully able to sit there and observe the outcome.*

Now there are those without autonomy, orphan souls who do not have the eye to penetrate the barrier: They just compare gain and loss, not only missing the point of the ancients but also burying their own selves. When you see with clear eyes, how can you suppress a laugh?

Do you understand the point? Highly refined pure gold shouldn't change color.

ZEN MASTER TONGXUAN SAID,

The two recluses keep the ultimate treasure hidden in their chests, waiting for the right people. Zhaozhou, moreover, is an ocean-faring merchant; rare are those who know the appropriate price.

TRANSLATOR'S COMMENTS

The Zen master here is the same Zhaozhou already met in the first koan (*No*) and the seventh koan ("Wash Your Bowl"). This "Testing Hermits" is a very important koan; it is generally considered notoriously difficult for the uninitiated to see into it.

To begin with, it is essential to understand the meaning of being a hermit in the context of Zen Buddhism.

As usual, this meaning is multifold. One point must be stressed in distinguishing the use of the term "hermit" in this Zen tradition from the way it is used in some other traditions, including secular traditions of common parlance.

A Zen hermit in the classical sense is not someone who wants to avoid the problems of the world and drops out of society.

In the outermost meaning of the technical language of ancient Zen, hermits were illuminated graduates of Zen schools who isolated themselves for a period of time in order to develop their transcendental insight and practical knowledge in such a way as to prepare them to reenter the ordinary human world in a very special state of balance. To be complete Zen masters, they needed to be effective communicators at some common level in order to contact society; yet they also needed to be free from personal nostalgia for the human condition in order to contribute to society a range of knowledge genuinely beyond the fluctuating and vulnerable subjectivity of ordinary human psychology with all of its anxieties and wishful thinking.

In spare technical terms, therefore, a Zen Buddhist "hermit" is someone who has attained nirvana and is thus inwardly beyond the world. The isolation of the hermit need not be grossly physical: "Seclusion" is a symbol and also a description of the psychological independence, both emotional and intellectual, that comes to the individual through the experience of nirvana.

So when Zhaozhou, who represents complete Zen mastery, poses the question "Is there? Is there?" to the hermits, in effect he asks them whether their nirvana is deep enough to empower them to go on the "living road" of objective reality.

Then when the hermits raise their fists, this can mean one of two things, each of which in turn may have two meanings. The reason, by the way, that koans like this may seem on analysis to have been constructed on mathematical principles is that they were indeed constructed to represent principles deriving from the same source as mathematics. *No Barrier* is one of the koan collections that shows this most clearly, although there is certainly little else but this fact being demonstrated in classical commentaries.

In any case, the reason there are two hermits in this story is to illustrate two categories of perspective. One perspective is the ineffability of the absolute: Nothing at all can really describe either nirvana or the immediate experience of suchness. In Zen jargon, this perspective is called "holding still." The second perspective is the interconnectedness of everything in a cosmic web of Life: The hermit's fist holds everything in its empty grip, because everything is in its place in one indivisible whole. In Zen jargon, this perspective is called "letting go."

The Zen master's reactions illustrate the dual level of possible meaning in each perspective. "A ship cannot moor where the water is shallow," he says, indicating that it is impossible to take on samsara effectively without sufficient depth of nirvana: In Zen, peace of mind is not just for your own enjoyment, but to help you work for the world unwearied. If the hermit was indicating "holding still" in nirvana, therefore, Zhaozhou's reply means to make sure of that stillness and not rise to any bait (like the bait the master just threw him with that question). If the hermit was indicating "letting go" in the infinite network of suchness, Zhaozhou's reply means to make sure your experience is real suchness and not a shallow subjective view of the world, which you have simply given a lofty title.

This orderly multiplicity of meaning is what Zen master Yun-an (pronounced Ywun-ahn) refers to as the "echo" in the words "a ship cannot moor where the water is shallow."

Turning to the other hermit in the koan, who naturally symbolizes another perspective or another way of looking at things, Zhaozhou says, to the same silent reply, "Can concede, can deny, can kill, can enliven." The terms "concede" and "enliven" refer to "letting go" into the infinite path of suchness, which is Life itself, set free. The terms "deny" and "kill" refer to "holding still" in the profound independence of nirvana, "not subject" to any mundane influence. These are the "barbs" in the statement, as Zen master Yun-an describes them.

In this case the Zen master says that whichever perspective you are absorbed in, it is crucial to be able to go back and forth freely in order to attain both ultimate liberation and objective compassion. Either perspective can kill you or bring you to life: The mythical "third eye" is nothing but the centered "Middle Way," a faculty of vision that so to speak hovers over the pivotal point at which one may plunge either into nirvana as such or thusness as such. This is not a one-time choice, as schismatic sectarians once believed; it takes place over and over again, even in the course of one day.

With this detailed explanation of the koan, I believe people will be able to understand the reasons for the comments made by Wumen and the other masters, in terms of the symbolism and scope of reference involved. The essential points may be summed up as follows. The "riddle" of this koan is not in a question of two anonymous but evidently specific persons winning and losing a contest of wits; it is in simultaneous perception of all the implications represented in a symbolic vignette. The point of this exercise is that this scenario contains an outline of the foundations and possibilities of conscious experience of life and death. In Zen, a Buddha is called a complete human being, with a complete mind: This means someone who has completely experienced the essence of life and death and therefore knows what they really mean and what possibilities are actually open to human awareness.

Therefore Wumen warns us not to get stuck on comparing better or worse, then also warns us not to conclude by this remark of his that there is no differentiation. As Yun-an says in the second paragraph of his comments, comparing in crude terms of gain and loss not only obscures the real point of the koan, but also occupies the mind wastefully. There are comparisons to make, nevertheless; but these comparisons cannot be resolved into a supposed choice between two individuals in a given case, as a superficial reading of the koan might suggest. The choice is among a range of fundamental possibilities, and it is a choice that is not fixed but *ongoing*, just as the four seasons are ongoing. And just like the four seasons, the totality of Zen teaching inspires and nurtures, and it also kills and reaps.

Zen is not a slapstick farce, or a competitive institution: People who take it this way show something about themselves, not about Zen. This is the point of Zen master Yun-an's "laugh" at those who "compare gain and loss." When Yun-an goes on to speak of pure gold, he refers to the purified Buddha-nature, the repository of all human possibilities, which Zhaozhou addresses in both hermits.

Zen master Tongxuan (pronounced Toong-shwen) pursues this Buddha-nature theme, showing how the story can be seen as both hermits representing one side of enlightenment, with Zhaozhou representing the "third eye" hovering over the pivotal working that can "set up" or "shut down," affirm or deny, proceed or withdraw, making deliberate choices according to needs in the course of living life through.

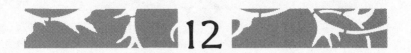

Calling the Master

Every day Ruiyan would call to himself, "Master!"
And he would answer himself, "Yes?"
Then he would say, "Be awake, be alert!"
"Yes."
"From now on, don't be fooled by anyone!"
"Yes, yes!"

WUMEN SAYS,
*Old Ruiyan sells himself and buys himself, playing out
so many spirit heads and ghost faces. Why? Listen!!
One who calls, one who answers, one who is alert, one
who is not fooled by others: If you cling to recognition,
as before you are not right. And if you imitate another,
everything is wild foxy interpretation.*

WUMEN'S VERSE
*When people studying the Way do not perceive reality,
It is just because they still recognize the conscious spirit;
It is the root of infinite eons of birth and death,
Yet the ignorant call it the original human being.*

TRANSLATOR'S COMMENTS

Ruiyan (pronounced Zrway-yen) lived in the ninth century. According to Zen records, many extraordinary tales were told of Ruiyan in his time, but were omitted from writings about him. The koan at hand is the best-known story featuring the image of this Zen master.

Ancient records state that Ruiyan used to sit quietly on a boulder all day long, and would call to himself thus every day. Framed in this way, the koan shows that Zen meditation is not idle or undirected sitting, but has a definite aim, as illustrated by Ruiyan's calls: to know the true self, to be awake and aware, and to be free from illusions and delusions developed by learned habits of association and thought.

Ruiyan's little drama exteriorizes the Zen quest for the purpose of illustration. Wumen's comment underscores the point that it all takes place within the self, and warns the seeker against two pitfalls. One is the danger of mistakenly recognizing the superficial personality for the real self; so Wumen says, "if you cling to recognition, as before you are not right." The other pitfall is to imitate the practice of the exercise without the inner spirit; so Wumen says, "if you imitate another, everything is wild foxy interpretation," meaning that it is just an arbitrary play of intellectual craft.

Wumen's verse comment also carries a traditional Zen caveat; in fact, it is an exact quotation of a classical statement on the subject. Here, the "conscious spirit" represents the subjective mind, which meditators who have practiced a little bit of thought-stopping may readily mistake for the real original mind of Zen.

This point is highlighted in another story about Ruiyan's Zen play. Someone came to one of the great contemporary masters and remarked, "Everyone plays with the mind, but Ruiyan is a bit better." This refers to the direct aim of the Zen effort written explicitly into Ruiyan's script.

The master rejoined, "Why don't you stay with him?" This means, in effect, "Why don't you put his method into practice?"

To this the questioner replied, "He has passed on," symbolically claiming to have himself completed and graduated from this exercise.

Zen masters don't let people make such claims without ascertaining their verity. This master asked, "Right now, can you call and get a response?" He wanted to see if the questioner had in fact embodied conscious realization of the real mind or the true self.

In the end there was no reply; the questioner had only been showing off. A later Zen master related this story and said, "All the Zen teachers in the world utter sayings on behalf of this questioner, much like neighbors helping the mourning at a funeral. But even if Ruiyan himself were to come forth, that would still be glaring eyes inside a coffin." Your answer to the Zen question, "Right now, can you call and get an answer?" has to be a genuine firsthand reflection of your own realization, not a contrived imitation of somebody else.

Deshan Carrying His Bowl

One day Zen master Deshan left the hall with his bowl in hand. He met Xuefeng, who asked him, "The bell and drum announcing the mealtime have not yet been sounded; where are you going with your bowl?"

Deshan immediately returned to his room.

Xuefeng told Yantou about this. Yantou said, "Even the great Deshan does not know the last word."

Hearing of this, Deshan had an assistant summon Yantou, whom he asked, "You don't agree with me?"

Yantou secretly revealed his intention, and Deshan dropped the subject.

The next day Deshan gave a lecture that turned out to be very different from usual. Yantou went to the front of the communal hall, where he clapped and laughed, saying, "How fortunate the old fellow understands the last word! After this no one in the world will be able to do anything to him."

WUMEN SAYS,

As far as the last word is concerned, neither Yantou nor Deshan had even dreamed of it. When you bring them up for examination, they're much like puppets on a stage.

WUMEN'S VERSE

If you know the first word,
Then you understand the last word;
The last and the first—
Are they not this one word?

ZEN MASTER BAO-EN SAID,

If you accept unrealities and take in echoes, you miss
Deshan. If you suppress the strong and help the weak, you
bury Yantou. I tell you frankly, for an example of the proverb,
"When the teacher is excellent, the apprentices are strong,"
credit goes to Deshan and his disciples Xuefeng and Yantou.
Expertise is demonstrated in the hands of experts; who knows
beyond the knowledge of connoisseurs?

ZEN MASTER YOUKE SAID,

Those who conceal an army to fight by night do not see
Deshan. Those who attack occupied territory by day can
hardly know Yantou. What they don't realize is that the bat-
tle commander picks fights by day, the watch commander
patrols the camp by night.

TRANSLATOR'S COMMENTS

Zen master Deshan (pronounced Duh-shahn) lived in the
ninth century. Xuefeng (pronounced Shweh-fung) and
Yantou (pronounced Yen-toe) were his Zen apprentices,
both of whom became exceptionally great Zen masters. In
Zen lore, Xuefeng ordinarily typifies diligence, while
Yantou typifies spontaneity.

Japanese masters considered this one of the most difficult

koans. The greatest difficulty in it is that it is not what it appears to be: like the eleventh koan, "Testing Hermits," this koan is an elaborate testing device. Part of the function of the koan's structure is to arouse doubt in the mind of the onlooker, in order to examine the doubt, the doubter, and the doubting.

Some say Yantou, who was enlightened long before Xuefeng even though both were in the circle of the grand master Deshan, was provoking an incident in order to help Xuefeng wake up, or to help Deshan help Xuefeng wake up.

Keizan, a great fourteenth-century Japanese Zen master, explains the story in an interesting way: "Deshan just accepts the flow, being as is. Yantou and Xuefeng scatter rubbish in the eye; playing at being adept, they turn out inept."

The identity of the "first word" and the "last word" refers to the identity of samsara and nirvana, or the relative and the absolute, or responsibility and freedom. A genuine understanding of either implies an understanding of both, and this story represents the interaction of partial and complete realization of these two facets of the total experience of awakeness.

Wumen's prose comment affirms that this koan is a didactic "play" illustrating a pivotal point in Zen awareness. He signals to us not to be misled by random associations the outward appearance may trigger. His poem refers to both union and unity of samsara and nirvana, within which total perspective each of the adepts in the story plays out a specific role as a signpost.

The comments of Zen master Bao-en (pronounced Bow-un) and Zen master Youke (pronounced Yo-kuh) are most enlightening. In Bao-en's terms, Deshan represents complete certainty, realization of the essence of reality; he will not quibble over secondary things and superficialities. Yantou represents the inspiring function of Zen, which challenges the self-imposed limits of subjective reality. The teacher and disciples together in the total interaction represent the whole operation of Zen teaching.

Youke says that those who think in contrived and contentious terms cannot see the point of this story. As with koan number eleven, "Testing Hermits," they only think in terms of who supposedly won and who supposedly lost. Thus a wealth of subtlety is completely lost to them.

In Youke's own colorful description, the "battle commander" who "picks fights by day" is first of all Deshan when he meanders down to the dining hall with his bowl before the formal announcement of mealtime; then it is Xuefeng when he confronts Deshan, and again when he reports this to Yantou; then it is Yantou, when he completes the circle by reporting Xuefeng's comment to Deshan, who now becomes the battle commander again by confronting Yantou and then giving a lecture completely different from usual. Finally Yantou again assumes the role of battle commander picking fights by making his last remarks in order to engage the attention of everyone else in the world on the complete transcendence of Deshan.

In the same way, the "watch commander" who "patrols the camp by night" is also Deshan, then Xuefeng, then Yantou, then Deshan, then Yantou, who finally asks us to take over for them. In order to be able to take over, we have to see for ourselves what Xuefeng was watching over, what Yantou was watching over, and what Deshan was watching over. The difficult part is that in order to do that, we need to have already accepted the night watch of calmly looking into ourselves for the firsthand experience of the essential mind that sees all independently: "Who knows beyond the knowledge of connoisseurs?"

Killing a Cat

Because the monks of the eastern and western halls were fighting over a cat, Master Nanquan picked it up and said, "If you can speak, I'll spare the cat. If not, I'll kill it."

No one replied, so Nanquan killed it.

That evening Zhaozhou came back from somewhere else and Nanquan told him what had happened. Zhaozhou then took off his sandals, put them on his head, and walked out.

Nanquan said, "Had you been here, you could have saved the cat."

WUMEN SAYS,
Tell me, what did Zhaozhou mean by putting his straw sandals on his head? If you can utter a pivotal word here, you will see how Nanquan's imperative was not carried out in vain. Otherwise, danger!

WUMEN'S VERSE
Had Zhaozhou been present,
He'd have executed the order in reverse,
Snatching the knife away,
Nanquan begging for his life.

ZEN MASTER ZHONGFENG BEN SAID,

Nanquan's sword is drawn from its jewel scabbard on account of unrest; Zhaozhou's medicine is taken from its precious jar in order to cure sickness. But even though that was fine for the time, nevertheless the way of the ancient Buddhas has disappeared.

TRANSLATOR'S COMMENTS

Nanquan (pronounced Nahn-chwen) was born in the eighth century and lived until the middle of the ninth century. He is considered one of the greatest classical masters, although relatively little of his teaching is used in traditional Zen lore. The reason for this apparent paradox is that Nanquan represents one of the most extraordinary combinations of high-mindedness and humility, of transcendent enlightenment and diligent effort; and little of his teaching can be practiced without these qualities. Therefore his effective legacy in most initiatory Zen lore is an icon of ultimate reality in the context of certain special stories representing absolute transcendence.

Zhaozhou has already appeared in the very first koan in this collection, where he uttered the famous *"No,"* another symbol of transcendence, and in the seventh koan, "Wash Your Bowl," which also has the meaning of transcending even transcendence. The historical Zhaozhou was actually a disciple of the historical Nanquan, so it is no coincidence that these two figures are iconographically very close in Zen lore. Both Nanquan and Zhaozhou were so high-minded that their historical lineage disappeared from the face of the earth in a very short time, but their quintessential reflections of enlightenment have been preserved for all time in Zen symbolism.

In the koan at hand, the cat represents the teaching, or any aspect of the teaching, including any aspect of reality uncovered by application of the teaching. The two factions of monks represent different points of view that have lost contact with a common ground.

Buddhist teaching loses its spiritual life when it is taken in a biased way. A typical example of this is when subjective understanding or application is made into an object of pride and attachment.

This kind of attachment results in contention and dispute, which dissipates energy and attention. This same energy and attention could otherwise be made available, as indeed required, for the objective application of the teaching to a real situation.

Zhaozhou's farcical act silently remarks that to be enslaved by something that originally was supposed to foster liberation is like being worn by a pair of shoes instead of wearing them.

Nanquan says that Zhaozhou would have saved the cat, because this is the very point he was trying to make to the disputatious monks: Ride the vehicle, don't be ridden by it. To ride the vehicle of Buddhism means to transcend human greed, aggression, and stupidity. To be ridden by the vehicle of Buddhism means to become pompous about piety—when you let ordinary human desire or ambition for spirituality or enlightenment increase the burden of your self-importance.

The meaning of Wumen's prose comment should already be obvious. That Nanquan's "imperative was not carried out in vain" means that his action draws a response, which at least allows bystanders to see. This refers to the demonstration of Zhaozhou, and to the understanding of the observant reader.

In Wumen's verse, he says that Zhaozhou would have

"executed the order in reverse, / snatching the knife away, / Nanquan begging for his life." Nanquan picked up the "knife" to separate disciples from their attachments to favorite points of view, so that they could be unemotional about spiritual teaching in order to see it clearly and objectively. Zhaozhou then snatched the same knife away and separated everyone from fixation on the outward form, or a personal interpretation, of the present act of teaching performed by Nanquan.

In case some may think Wumen's inclusion of Nanquan here is random or trivial, consider the historical fact that many seekers of Zen Buddhism have actually labored at length over the supposed issue of whether or not Nanquan actually took the life of a living being in this story. This is not a morality play, not because there are no relevant morals in Buddhism, but because those morals are not in any way in question here, just as the ontology of animal Buddha-nature was not in question in the first koan.

It is not that there is no use in irrelevant nonquestions supposedly arising from Zen koans; but their use is in the illustration of irrelevancy and meaninglessness, not in elucidating the koans. The comments of Zen master Zhongfeng (pronounced Joong-fung) make this eminently clear: Nanquan's "sword" is his Zen method of cutting through the webs and tangles of attachments and confusions; Zhaozhou's "medicine" is his Zen method of curing the sickness of blindness and stupidity. Zhongfeng says that the one is drawn on account of unrest, the other brought out in order to cure sickness: In other words, these teaching setups are only expedients, designed to meet the needs of a specific type of situation.

Thus he goes on to say "that was fine for the time," meaning that the efficacy of an expedient is in its timeliness. Yet he concludes, "the way of the ancient Buddhas has disappeared," cautioning the reader that fixation of attention on the external face of the acts of the Zen masters will obscure the real point of the koan, which is in the living application of insight. This is also, naturally, a warning against ignorant imitation. That is especially true of a koan like this "killing a cat" story, whose surface content tends to baffle almost everyone. This baffling quality can lend itself to perversions and abuses like mystification and charlatanism.

In reality, a koan is like a lens that focuses a specific insight. The purpose is to see through the lens, not look at its outward appearance. The "way of the ancient Buddhas" means eternal truth, not temporal form. This is the "gold-testing stone" of Zen.

15

Threescore Blows

When Dongshan came to study with Yunmen, the teacher asked him, "Where have you come from?"

Dongshan said, "Chadu."

Yunmen asked, "Where did you spend the summer?"

Dongshan said, "At Baoci monastery in Hunan."

Yunmen asked, "When did you leave there?"

Dongshan said, "August twenty-fifth."

Yunmen said, "I forgive you threescore blows."

The next day Dongshan went to Yunmen and asked, "Yesterday you forgave me threescore blows; I do not know where my error was."

Yunmen said, "You rice bag! Jiangxi, Hunan, and you still go on this way!"

At this Dongshan was greatly enlightened.

WUMEN SAYS,

If Yunmen had given some of his own provisions at that time, enabling Dongshan to have another road of living potential, then his school would not have become extinct.

One night Dongshan was in the ocean of right and wrong; the next morning he went again, and was given an explanation. Dongshan was immediately enlightened, but he still wasn't quick.

Now I ask you, should Dongshan receive the threescore blows, or should he not? If you say he should, then all the plants and trees should be beaten. If you say he should not, then Yunmen was talking nonsense.

WUMEN'S VERSE
A lion teaches its cub the secret of the wanderling;
When it tries to leap forward, immediately it's flipped.
An unexpected second try gets right to the point;
The earlier arrow was still light, the later one went deep.

ZEN MASTER FUSHAN SAID,
Hold the universe still, and even Buddhas and Zen masters have no way to get in; throw open the rivers and seas, and fish and dragons get room to swim.

FAREN NING SAID,
Had it not been for his diligence at the end, Dongshan would have fallen into a pit of quicksand, never to get out. Then again, it was just because of his diligence at the end that Dongshan fell into a pit of quicksand, never to get out.

TRANSLATOR'S COMMENTS

Yunmen (pronounced Ywun-mun) died in 949. He was one of the greatest classical masters, not only profoundly enlightened but also an extraordinary genius with an amazing versatility of mind. His scope of attainment of the awakening described in the Flower Ornament Scripture, traditionally considered the original teaching of Buddhism, was truly outstanding. This Dongshan (pronounced Doong-shahn) was one of more than eighty enlightened disciples of the great master Yunmen.

The koan at hand is about suchness, or being-as-is. Yunmen is a perfect icon for suchness koans, because of his dazzling expressions of the most sophisticated level of realization, known in comprehensive Flower Ornament Buddhism as simultaneous "interpenetration of all phenomena" and "noninterference among all individual phenomena." This vision cannot be completely explained in words; its effect is perception of universal harmony within the totality of the universe.

At first, Yunmen's conversation with Dongshan in this koan seems to touch on everyday matters. In Zen Buddhist iconography, everyday matters are everyday matters and also symbols of being-as-is. The distinction between everyday matters and being-as-is lies in the subjectivity or objectivity of the observer, so the Zen master needs to test to see whether the seeker's perception is conditioned and subjective or direct and objective; whether the seeker only sees the mundane aspect of suchness, or whether the seeker also sees the suchness of the mundane.

By the end of the third round, Yunmen and Dongshan are even. No one can tell whether the seeker only sees the sacred as mundane, or also sees the mundane as sacred. Therefore Yunmen sets another trap and "forgives him threescore blows."

The number three in Zen generally refers to three steps that lead from ordinary subjective reality to the suchness of objective reality. The first is mental detachment. This does not mean resistance or opposition to mental activities, as often imagined by intellectuals, but rather nonattachment. The purpose of detachment from mental talk is to open up a window for subtler faculties of perception that usually lie dormant behind the noisier and more colorful facade of thoughts, imaginings, and ideas.

The second step is detachment from detachment. This does not mean resumption of former habits of thought, but rather enlivening newly awakened insights and learning to relate to the world in awakened ways.

The third step is to refrain from forming conceptions of detachment or detachment from detachment, so that the process does not degenerate into an indirect intellectual exercise.

These are the "threescore blows" that Yunmen "forgives" Dongshan. The seeker who has gone through them will understand his meaning; the seeker who has not finished the last one will wonder why the teacher speaks of "forgiving," because he still has a tendency to rationalize his relationship with suchness.

As it turns out, Dongshan got "caught" by Yunmen's "hook." Nevertheless, we still cannot tell whether he is an innocent playing innocent, an imbecile being an imbecile, or a self-approved seeker claiming to spontaneous and unselfconscious union with being-as-is.

Therefore the Zen master Yunmen tests him again. Naming some areas famous for the many Zen teachers then active there—and indeed the place the seeker just said he had come from was itself a famous teaching center—Yunmen says, in effect, if you are a seeker who is claiming to have found the reality of suchness, what are you doing here? Why are you still seeking, using up the alms of the faithful, if you have in fact attained the aim?

It might be said that Yunmen wanted to see whether Dongshan only saw the samsara or mundane aspect of suchness, or whether he also saw the heart of nirvana in that samsara. That is the criterion of real suchness. My teacher used to say that Yunmen was truly magical: At the same time as he tossed a bucket of samsara at the seeker and made it work like nirvana, he also drenched him with a bucket of nirvana while making it look like samsara.

Wumen's comments on this koan are also very clever. He says that Yunmen did not give Dongshan some of his own provisions. This means that Yunmen did not show his own realization of suchness, which would have enabled the seeker to "have another road of living potential" beyond nirvana. As it was, Yunmen simply showed Dongshan the heart of nirvana within knowledge of samsara, causing him to be greatly enlightened in this sense but not giving him any indication or guidance in matters of the higher possibilities of consciousness beyond this stage.

That is why Wumen says indirectly that Yunmen's school became extinct. Although this is historically true, and it was true of most of the exceptional classical Zen masters, the historical fact is here just a symbol; the meaning of this remark is that this koan is about seeing the heart of nirvana within samsara. Wumen's comments up to this point are not criticisms of Yunmen or his method, even though they are deliberately presented that way in order to "catch" superficial literalists for the demonstrative effect achieved thereby; Wumen's comments are a precise technical description of the specific meaning and function of this particular koan.

Turning the focus of attention to Dongshan, Wumen says that one "night," or in his state of ignorance, he was in "the ocean of right and wrong," or the abyss of subjectively biased discriminatory thinking. Wumen acknowledges that the ordinary world turned into true suchness with the dawn of his awakening "the next morning." Nevertheless, Wumen says, recalling the standpoint originally expressed by Yunmen himself, if Dongshan had really been "quick," if he actually had immediate and direct experience of suchness, he wouldn't have needed to approach Yunmen in the first place.

Finally, Wumen poses a question to the reader. We already know that the question of whether or not Dongshan deserved the blows depends on something else: Now Wumen has us look at that something else. "If you say he should, then all the plants and trees should be beaten"— when you practice the three-step Zen progression from ordinary subjective reality to directly experienced objective suchness, the process takes in everything everywhere, at all times.

"If you say he should not," Wumen goes on, referring to the time when application of the teaching has taken effect and the resulting return to essential nature is complete, "then Yunmen was talking nonsense," because there is no sense in clinging to the means once the end is attained, provided the end is itself real. This remark contains a key to Yunmen's testing procedure as well as a typical warning to the reader not to get distracted by the superficial appearance of the procedure.

In Wumen's verse, the "lion" is a traditional symbol for enlightened consciousness. It is said that the roar of a lion bursts the brain of a jackal, meaning that enlightenment silences delusive thoughts.

The "secret of the wanderling" is the Zen question that starts off the koan, "Where have you come from?" This question is posed in every possible sense, to see the level at which an individual seeker interprets it. It is a test of whether the seeker is conscious of the ultimate source of being as well as a test of what the seeker has experienced.

"When it tries to leap forward, immediately it's flipped." Dongshan came on as if he was present in consciousness of being-as-is; Yunmen let him leap, then flipped him with talk of punishment and forgiveness.

"An unexpected second try gets right to the point." Having been flipped around like this by Yunmen, Dongshan was enabled to make a fresh approach, without presumption on conceptual clichés, trying to get to the truth directly.

"The earlier arrow was still light, the later one went deep." The first arrow was "I forgive you threescore blows," which aroused doubt and broke through complacence. The second arrow was "You rice bag!" which shot right to the heart of pride to turn it into the heart of nirvana.

I have gone into such detail with Wumen's comments on this case in particular to emphasize the point that his remark about the extinction of Yunmen's school is meant symbolically. As a point of historical fact, in spite of its extraordinary character, Yunmen's school lasted for a very long time, and after it passed out of view its teaching was inherited by another school, the Linji school. As a graduate of this latter school, Wumen here shows his ability to interpret Yunmen teachings and even to present them in a brilliantly clever manner, as was characteristic of the lofty tone of the Yunmen school of Zen.

The comments of other Zen masters on this koan are similarly artful. Fushan (pronounced Foo-shahn) summarizes all the issues of the whole story in penetrating detail by making full use of the dual meanings in the Zen terms "hold still" and "throw open."

Fushan begins by saying, "Hold the universe still, and even Buddhas and Zen masters have no way to get in." When the expression "hold still" is taken in its sense of fixation, this saying means that when you cling to superficial appearances it is impossible to awaken to suchness as it really is. This image stands for the seeker Dongshan in the beginning, insofar as he symbolizes complacent identification of ordinary consciousness with perception of being-as-is.

In contrast, when "hold still" is taken in its other sense of remaining in the stillness of absolute nirvana, Fushan's statement means that no thoughts or conceptions apply to that state, not even ideas or images of Buddhahood or Zen mastery. This image stands for the master Yunmen reproving attachment to "suchness," turning the focus of attention to the heart of nirvana within knowledge of suchness.

Fushan then goes on to say, "Throw open the rivers and seas, and fish and dragons get room to swim." This also can have two meanings, referring to the states or principles represented by the seeker and the master.

When "throw open" is taken in the sense of conceding the all-inclusive nature of suchness, Fushan's saying represents Yunmen going along with Dongshan and "forgiving" him, letting him be as he is in order to see whether he is a "fish" (ordinary person) or a "dragon" (illuminate).

Then again, when "throw open" is taken in the sense of letting go of attachment to fixed attitudes and ideas, thus realizing the "open" or fluid nature of reality itself, Fushan's saying represents Dongshan attaining enlightenment and liberation on realizing the heart of nirvana within the experience of suchness.

The comment of Zen master Faren (pronounced Fahzren) likens being-as-is to a "pit of quicksand," because suchness is at bottom what the clinging mind turns into the prison of the ordinary world. Dongshan's "diligence at the end" refers to his response to Yunmen's challenge, without which doubt he would not have attained the heart of nirvana and become enlightened.

Appearing to turn things around, but simply completing the teaching, Faren adds that it is precisely by means of profound experience of nirvana that one can manage being-as-is to the furthest possible degree. This practical capacity is a representation of a major saint in Buddhism, called a bodhisattva (pronounced bode-hee-sot-twuh), or enlightening being, who keeps on transcending in order to keep up dedication, thus able to be inwardly free even while working for the liberation of the world right there in the midst of its bondage.

As for Dongshan, it might be said that his was another case of an awakening illustrated by the saying, "Had he known the lamp was fire, the meal would have been cooked already." To see the point of the "threescore blows," please reflect on this saying.

16

Putting on a Formal Vestment at the Sound of a Bell

Yunmen said, "The world is so wide, so vast; why put on a formal vestment at the sound of a bell?"

WUMEN SAYS,
Whenever you investigate Zen and study the Way, it is urgent to avoid pursuing sound and chasing form. Even if you realize the Way on hearing sound, or understand the mind on seeing form, this is still ordinary; you do not yet know how Zen learners ride on sound and enclose form, everywhere clear, every experience sublime.

But even so, tell me: Does sound come to the ear, or does the ear go to sound? Even if echoes and silence are both forgotten, when you reach this, how do you understand verbally? If you use your ears to listen, it will be hard to understand; only when you hear sound through your eyes will you be close.

WUMEN'S VERSE

Understand, and things are all one;
If you don't understand, there are myriad distinctions, a
* thousand differences.*
When you don't understand, things are all one;
Understand, and there are myriad distinctions, a thousand
* differences.*

ZEN MASTER GUSHAN'S VERSE

The formal vestment goes on at the sound of a bell;
The whole world cannot hide the appearance of a monk.
But if you see by way of form, or seek by way of sound,
The Buddha's successor, our teacher, was a fake.

TRANSLATOR'S COMMENTS

This is the same Zen master Yunmen encountered in the fifteenth koan. He was especially noted for his skill in expressing many meanings simultaneously within apparently simple utterances.

It is recorded that Yunmen spoke the words of this koan on hearing the sound of the temple bell. "Putting on a formal vestment at the sound of a bell" symbolizes acknowledgment of purposeful order. In domestic terms, it is like tying your shoes and buttoning your shirt, cooking meals and washing the dishes, watering the plants and feeding the animals.

The point of this koan follows the preceding one. The "vastness" of the world to which Yunmen refers is the experience of nirvana in the essence of mind. From the point of view of absolute nirvana, all order is relative, so the mind should be open and fluid if one is to experience the fullest possible extent of that portion of infinity accessible to consciousness. The danger of misunderstanding or exaggerating this point of view, however, is to slip into habits of ignorance, heedlessness, and denial masquerading as realization of emptiness and transcendence. The point of this koan, therefore, is to examine the transcendence of transcendence, which means emergence from quiescent nirvana into perception of suchness as a cosmic web of events and processes.

Yunmen's question is not about one particular order, but any particular order and its relationship to the essence of order. It is a reminder to be mindful when reemerging from absorption in the ineffable absolute into the plane of order, to be sure one is not projecting subjective ideas based on old habits.

In the temptation to think of order exclusively as a specific order there is a typical Zen hook, designed to show whether a particular individual identifies the temporal form of a particular order with the eternal reality of order itself. In some sense everyone perceives some aspect of reality; illusion consists of imagining this limited perception to be the whole of reality; delusion consists of fabricated ideas and rationalizations filling the gaps between fragments of partial views of reality.

Wumen's prose comment is a study in balance: He tells the seeker not to be obsessed with formalities, and yet not to become disorderly or negligent. In the second paragraph, Wumen gives directions for meditation to bring this Zen to life. "Does sound come to the ear, or does the ear go to sound?" In other words, are you "receiving" suchness as it is, or are you projecting what you expect? When "echoes and silence are both forgotten" is when you transcend the world and transcend transcendence; then you see the infinity of reality, not in fragments but as a whole, because you are seeing with your whole body and whole being.

Wumen's verse on this koan is unusually complicated. It is most easily understood when broken down line by line:

"Understand, and all things are one." Unity realized through understanding refers to a) direct perception and b) logical understanding of the interdependence of all things, which is the basis of order and causality.

"If you don't understand, there are myriad distinctions, a thousand differences." Diversity experienced through not understanding refers to a) blindness to unity of essence by fixation on external appearances, and b) preoccupation of attention with subjective discriminations.

"When you don't understand, things are all one." In a mundane sense, this refers to unity experienced through not understanding as reflecting everything in a fixed worldview. In a transcendental sense, it refers to unity experienced through not understanding as seeing the totality of things in holistic perception without subjective judgments.

"Understand, and there are myriad distinctions, a thousand differences." Diversity experienced through understanding refers to the capacity of objective analysis and discernment of practical differences.

A further refinement of the story in this koan underscores the message that stagnation is to be avoided in the ever-transcending path of Zen. In the most extensive book on Yunmen it is also recorded that the monks in Yunmen's audience did not say anything, so the master himself said, chiding them for their silence, "On a short stretch of riverbank there are a lot of clams." Observing that no one gave evidence of any vision beyond the conventional, Zen master Wu-an (pronounced Woo-ahn) said of this scene,

On a short stretch of riverbank, many are the clams:
Once the sun comes out, their mouths all open.
Although their ordinary guts are revealed,
When have falcons ever come pursuing the smell?

The return of the Zen master to the ordinary world after transcendental experience of nirvana does not mean complacent acceptance of half-truths. The aftermath of awakening is awakeness: Those who have just awakened cannot assume that their sobriety is necessarily complete, and that they have become fully liberated from their former "dream" habits of thought.

Finally, the verse of Zen master Gushan summarizes the point, showing how the formal robe symbolizes the whole world of order, structure, and form, yet reminding everyone that the Buddha, the one who is Awake, is not identified with the clothing of form. Reproduction of form can only produce imitations of form, not the living source of all form in itself. Thus Gushan concludes by saying in effect that an imitation Buddha is by definition a "fake."

17

The National Teacher's Three Calls

The National Teacher called his assistant three times, and three times the assistant responded. The National Teacher said, "I had thought I was disappointing you. Actually it is you who are disappointing me."

WUMEN SAYS,

When the National Teacher called three times, his tongue fell to the ground; when the assistant answered three times, he spoke out luminously. The National Teacher, old of years and lonely at heart, held the ox's head to let it feed, but his assistant wouldn't take him up on it; fine food is not a suitable meal for the satiated.

Now tell me, where is the disappointment?

When a country is clean, talented people are valued. When a family is rich, the children are haughty.

The iron stocks have no opening, yet he wants the man to
  put them on:
The burden extends to descendants, not to be lightly
  dismissed.
If you want to be able to uphold the school,
You must go on to climb a sword mountain in your bare
  feet.

TRANSLATOR'S COMMENTS

National Teacher was a title of honor given to teachers of the emperor. A number of distinguished Zen monks received this title, but the most famous National Teacher in classical Zen lore was the great Huizhong (pronounced Hway-joong), who lived in the eighth century.

The koan at hand is a very famous one. It centers around the notion that the original mind and being-as-is are natural realities that cannot be taught or transmitted in the literal sense, but only realized by what is known as "teacherless knowledge," or direct firsthand experience of reality. Therefore this is also one of the koans that test realization of suchness, to see if it is superficial or deep, subjective or objective.

In the original story, the word for "disappoint" can be read to "let down" in the colloquial sense, or to betray, to turn against. There are many nuances in this koan.

According to one way of interpretation, the metaphorical "disappointment" or "betrayal" in this case is the suggestion implicit in the calling and answering that "there is something," which seemingly could compromise the transcendence and freedom of Zen. By calling attention to this, the teacher counsels people not to become so attached to the framework of study that they lose the real Zen content.

Another way of seeing the story is on the other side of the same coin: Zen masters have to teach their disciples not to chase their own imaginations; they have to teach them "nothing," as it were, so that they can unlearn the preconceived ideas that veil them from direct enlightenment. Therefore the master says ironically, "I thought I hadn't taught you anything; now I see you haven't learned anything."

Yet another way to view the story is to see that the teacher was testing the assistant, to see if he had any hidden doubts that would make him vulnerable to being "hooked." When the assistant simply acknowledged the event and remained where he was, he showed that he had attained fulfillment and was inwardly at peace. The teacher's final statement was then a recognition that the assistant had passed the test by foiling the trick.

In his prose commentary, Wumen gives a technical description of the points covered in the koan. He seems to chide the National Teacher, saying his "tongue fell to the ground," which means in Zen code, "Don't depend on anything, and don't take your ordinary perceptions for ultimate reality." Then Wumen praises the assistant, saying he "spoke out luminously," meaning that his "three responses" were complete affirmation of reality, be it ultimate, relative, or imagined.

Wumen goes on to make a gesture of ridicule toward the National Teacher's role again, portraying his calls as attempts to force-feed Zen to his assistant, who is no longer in need. As usual, this is a symbolic representation of a general principle, which states that the teaching is set up according to the situation, in response to the needs of the seeker. When the ailment is cured, goes the Zen proverb, the medicine is taken away. Thus Wumen says, "Fine food is not a suitable meal for the satiated."

As he often does, Wumen concludes his prose comments with a challenge. "When a country is clean, talented people are valued" refers to the National Teacher calling his apprentice; "when a family is rich, the children are haughty" refers to the apprentice answering his teacher. Where is the disappointment?

By now it will be obvious that the meaning of the National Teacher is in the power of his words to engage the doubt of the reader. When you know where the disappointment is, there is no more disappointment.

The last lines of both Wumen's prose and verse commentaries also voice traditional warnings about complacency and aloofness masquerading as genuine transcendence, which is not compromised even by intimate involvement in works in the world. The conclusion of Wumen's verse places particular emphasis on realizing the infinity of suchness, and the consequent endlessness of practical adaptation to its flow. The great Yunmen said, "Where does the assistant disappoint the National Teacher? Even to pulverize one's bones and shatter one's body would not be enough to pay back his debt."

Three Pounds

A monk asked Master Dongshan, "What is Buddha?"
Dongshan said, "Three pounds of burlap."

WUMEN SAYS,
Dongshan had learned a bit of clam Zen: He reveals his
guts the minute he opens his lips. But tell me, do you see
Dongshan?

WUMEN'S VERSE
He thrusts out three pounds of burlap;
The words are close, the intent even closer.
Those who come talking of right and wrong
Are therefore right and wrong people.

TRANSLATOR'S COMMENTS

Zen master Dongshan in this koan is the same one who attained enlightenment in the fifteenth koan, "Threescore Blows."

The present koan illustrates the kind of consciousness that Buddhists call the "great mirror knowledge," which is direct perception of being-as-is, reflection of suchness without subjective projections. Because it is impartial and objective, this kind of consciousness or "knowledge" is represented as being like a mirror. This mirrorlike awareness is one of four fundamental types of knowledge realized by Buddhas.

As usual, Wumen's comment seems to be a quip. He calls Dongshan's realization "clam Zen," in that you can see everything inside the minute he opens up, just as you can see inside a clam when it opens. This is a simple description of what the mirror knowledge is like: The whole panorama of immediate reality is reflected the instant the eye of this knowledge opens. Insofar as Wumen's remark does contain a kind of irony, the point is that this knowledge is only one aspect of enlightenment.

Thus Wumen's question "Do you see Dongshan?" is two-pronged. In one sense, the question is whether or not we mistake an image in the mirror for the mirror itself. In another sense, the question is whether we take one aspect of enlightenment for the whole.

In his verse comment, Wumen says, "The words are close, the intent even closer." The direct experience of suchness is "closer" to reality than any description. "Those who come talking of right and wrong," Wumen goes on, referring to those whose attention is fixed on the image and do not see the mirror, "are therefore right and wrong people," because all they see when they do this are reflections of their own ideas.

There is a detailed description of typical subjective views of this koan by the great Zen master Yuanwu (pronounced Ywen-woo), who lived a hundred years before Wumen and included the same koan in his own collection of classical lore, called *The Blue Cliff Record*:

> Many people base their understanding on the words and say that Dongshan was in the storehouse at the time weighing out hemp or burlap when the monk questioned him, and therefore he answered in this way. Some say that when Dongshan is asked about one thing he answers about another. Some say that since you are Buddha and yet you still go asking about Buddha, Dongshan answers this in a roundabout way. And there's yet another type of dead men who say that the three pounds of burlap is itself Buddha. These interpretations have nothing to do with it.

The most sophisticated comment on this popular koan comes from Zen master Tianbao (pronounced Tyen-bao), who cites a traditional teaching to "explain" in terms of three levels of reality: absolute reality, relative reality, and conceptually imagined reality. "To make rope of the hemp is still okay," the Zen master says, "but how can it be right to construe the rope as a snake?"

A classical Buddhist metaphor describes the relationship among these levels of reality by means of a story about a man who sees a piece of rope lying across his path at night. Unable to see clearly in the darkness, the man mistakes the rope for a snake and fears he may be bitten. Even though it is only a piece of rope, the man's distress is as real to him as the idea, or misperception, of the "snake."

Similarly, reality as conceptually imagined is like the

"snake"—something is there, but not as we imagine. Relative reality is like the "rope"—when we stop clinging to our conceptual descriptions, we can see suchness unadorned. Ultimate reality is the fact that the rope is not only not a snake, it is not even a "rope"—it is only a bundle of fibers.

The last distinction is very fine. The resolution into fiber represents the final analysis symbolically, not literally. Buddhist insight penetrates everything, so there is no element that is absolute. All descriptions of reality are only mental constructions, yet some descriptions are relatively truer than others. When it comes to ineffable absolute truth, even our perception of objective reality can never be total and complete.

So nothing can really be said to capture the experience of the ultimate truth in words, and the purity of this insight remains untouched in the mirror knowledge of Buddhas. Tianbao suggests that when we return from the experience of absolute nirvana that opens up the mirror knowledge, and attend to the differentiated aspect of the suchness seen by this knowledge, this attention to differentiation is cultivated for the purpose of developing analytic and practical knowledge, two other basic aspects of enlightened knowledge.

In this work it is essential to distinguish between the relatively true and the relatively false. As the Zen proverb says, you cannot harvest beans by planting wheat. That is why it is "still okay" to "make rope of the hemp," because that is objectively true on the relative plane; but "how can it be right to construe the rope as a snake," which could only be true in subjective imagination?

Let me conclude with a brief statement and a challenge from Zen master Jinsu (pronounced Jin-soo), who slyly alludes to the nature and limitations of the mirrorlike awareness as experienced in isolation, without the other fundamental aspects of enlightened knowledge: "If you can understand here," he says, "it is easy to see Dongshan, but hard to see your own self." Then he asks us why: "Once you have seen Dongshan, why don't you see yourself?" How can the front of a mirror reflect the back of the mirror itself?

The Normal Is the Way

Zhaozhou asked Nanquan, "What is the Way?"

Nanquan said, "The normal mind is the Way."

Zhaozhou asked, "Can it be approached deliberately?"

Nanquan said, "If you try to aim for it, you thereby turn away from it."

Zhaozhou said, "If one does not try, how can one know it is the Way?"

Nanquan said, "The Way is not in the province of knowledge, yet not in the province of unknowing. Knowledge is false consciousness, unknowing is indifference. If you really arrive at the inimitable Way, it is like space, empty and open; how can you insist on affirmation and denial?"

At these words, Zhaozhou was suddenly enlightened.

WUMEN SAYS,
Questioned by Zhaozhou, Nanquan simply crumbled and melted; he was unable to provide an explanation. As for Zhaozhou, even granting that he was enlightened, he still had to study for thirty years.

WUMEN'S VERSE

In spring there are a hundred flowers, in autumn there is
  the moon;
In summer there are cool breezes, in winter there is snow.
If no idle matters hang on your mind,
Then it is a good season in the human world.

ZEN MASTER JINGSHAN SAID,

The ancient spilled his guts all at once. The sky-scraping fal-
con should take advantage of the time; the tired fish resting in
the shallows wastes the effort to stir up waves.

ZEN MASTER FOJIAN'S VERSE

If you want to know the normal Way,
Trust nature spontaneously.
When you row a boat, you need to raise the oars;
When you ride a horse, you apply the crop.
If you get hungry, obtain some food;
And you should sleep when tired.
All is attained through conditions,
Yet what is attained is not a condition.

ZEN MASTER GUSHAN'S VERSE

If you think the normal mind is the Way,
You produce more ramifications on top of ramifications.
If you have taken off the sweaty shirt sticking to your flesh,
Given a call you find eyebrows atop your eyes.

TRANSLATOR'S COMMENTS

Nanquan and Zhaozhou have already been seen working together in the fourteenth koan, "Killing a Cat." The present koan is represented as the story of one of Zhaozhou's major awakenings, indicating its importance.

The essential point to remember in handling this koan is that the term "normal" here is a technical Zen usage. The early Japanese Zen master Dogen lamented the degeneration of Zen stemming from misunderstanding the expression "normal mind" or the saying "this mind is Buddha" to mean the ordinary mentality with its conditioned habits of thought. This is the crux of the issue in this koan, which should be examined very closely as a technical description of the normal mind as it is groomed and experienced in Zen.

Wumen's opening remark is also a technical description, which is as usual put in the form of a jibe for fools to fool with and thus demonstrate their own foolery, saving the teacher Wumen all that extra work. When he says that Nanquan couldn't provide an explanation, Wumen affirms that the experience of the normal mind, which is nothing but intimacy with being-as-is, cannot be described in words because of the limited nature of words themselves as compared with the infinity of suchness and the subtlety of the essence of mind itself.

Turning attention to Zhaozhou, Wumen remarks that he "still had to study for thirty more years" after this enlightenment. This is a typically indirect way of saying that there is further development after awakening. Once you recover the unconditioned consciousness of the pristine normal mind, then you turn from spontaneous absorption in the unity of suchness to precise awareness of the differentiations within suchness, so that you may be "not blind to causality."

After realizing the timeless absolute, you return to the temporal world. To "study for thirty years" means that realization is not to be maintained at its simplest and crudest level, but should be developed to encompass all aspects of relative reality as well as absolute truth. As in the preceding koan, Wumen stresses the need for completely rounded and mature enlightenment that encompasses all aspects of enlightened knowledge.

So as usual, Wumen is not talking about Zhaozhou; this story is just a representation of an issue that concerns everyone by virtue of being conscious. The remarks of Zen master Jingshan affirm that the koan is about a very fundamental and pervasive realization, and charges those who are capable, the "falcons," with the inherent obligation to awaken this Buddha-nature.

At the same time, Jingshan reminds the intellectual faculty not to try to think its way to ineffable enlightenment. He says that ordinary thoughts and conceptions, "tired fish resting in the shallows," cannot come to grips with true reality, and only call useless attention to themselves, thus "wasting the effort to stir up waves."

The verse of Zen master Fojian (pronounced Fwaw-jyen) is also extremely enlightening in spite of its apparent simplicity. The critical points to watch are in the last two lines. "All is attained through conditions" means that even though Buddha-nature is by definition natural, it still needs to be cultivated, because consciousness can be conditioned. "Yet what is attained is not a condition" means that the essence of flexibility and openness of spontaneous awareness is not identified with anything it may perceive or any function it may potentiate. This is the pivotal point of freedom in Zen.

Finally, the verse of Zen master Gushan underscores the traditional warning not to mistake ordinary conceptual consciousness for the "normal mind" of Zen. Using classical metaphors, Gushan affirms that it is necessary to strip the mind of arbitrarily conditioned habits of thought ("take off the sweaty shirt sticking to your flesh") in order to experience the suchness of being-as-is ("find eyebrows atop your eyes"). This is precisely what Wumen means when he concludes his verse comment with the lines, "If no idle matters hang on your mind, / then it is a good season in the human world"—only when you are not caught up in subjective imagination can you see suchness as it really is.

20

People of Great Power

Master Songyuan said, "Why is it that someone of great power cannot lift a foot?"

He also said, "Speaking out is not a matter of the tongue."

WUMEN SAYS,

Even if you get it right away, you should come to me and get a painful beating. Why? Listen!! If you want to discern real gold, see it in fire.

WUMEN'S VERSE

Lifting a foot, one stamps over the ocean;
Lowering the head, one looks down upon the heavens:
The whole body has nowhere to stay;
Please follow up with another line.

ZEN MASTER XUTANG'S VERSE

Power cannot lift aloft, let me tell you;
Why bother to whip a topflight horse?
With one leap sail into the thirty-six open skies;
When you arrive, your ordinary bones will turn immortal.

TRANSLATOR'S COMMENTS

Songyuan (pronounced Soong-ywen) was a thirteenth-century Zen master. Among his spiritual descendants was the distinguished Japanese pilgrim Dai-Ō, one of the founders of Zen in Japan.

The koan at hand refers to the experience of total absorption in the unity of being. Someone in this state "cannot lift a foot" because the "whole body" of this awareness fills the universe. Songyuan also says, "Speaking out is not a matter of the tongue," because this awareness can only be expressed through the whole being and is therefore literally indescribable in the language of ordinary conceptions.

Wumen's prose comment may be even more cryptic than usual. When he says that you should get a "painful beating" even if you apprehend suchness at once, this "beating" symbolizes the impact of ongoing experience of the infinite path of being-as-is. Enlightenment is not just a momentary flash of insight into the essence of mind and the suchness of reality: After you wake up, then you have to face the day. This so-called painful beating is the process of "facing the day" after you have awakened.

Having said this, Wumen suddenly becomes crystal clear and almost completely explicit: Genuine realization of Buddha-nature, in which the unity of nirvana and samsara becomes an evident reality, is tested and refined in the "fire" of this "painful beating" that is nothing but "not being blind to causality."

In his verse, Wumen begins by describing the vastness of this consciousness of cosmic unity. Then he uses that to open up the way to see the boundlessness and infinity of the cosmos of reality. In the end all he can do is let us see for ourselves.

Finally, the verse of Zen master Xutang (pronounced Shyw-tahng), who was the teacher of the Japanese Zen pilgrim Dai-Ō, affirms that this process of Zen realization is not a human invention but a natural law. Thus it occurs spontaneously when you follow its inherent pattern.

According to this natural law, which is also studied in Taoism, "power cannot lift aloft," in the sense that spiritual transformation cannot be forced; so "Why bother to whip a topflight horse?" The "topflight horse" is the Buddha-nature, the essence of mind itself, which is of the same essence as enlightenment and thus can "with one leap sail into the thirty-six open skies," a Taoist term for the infinite vastness of awakened consciousness. He concludes that "When you arrive, your ordinary bones turn immortal." When you awaken, the world and everything in it will be found to have turned into suchness itself.

 **21**

Yunmen's Turd

A monk asked Yunmen, "What is Buddha?"
Yunmen said, "A dry turd."

WUMEN SAYS,
Of Yunmen it could be said that "when the house is
poor, it's hard to get even a simple meal together; when
things are busy, there's no time to write." There is a
tendency to try to support schools with this dry turd; so
you can see the state of affairs in Buddhism.

WUMEN'S VERSE
A flash of lightning,
A flint struck spark;
If you blink your eyes,
You've already missed it.

ZEN MASTER LI-AN SAID,
A statement that startles the crowd is indeed a statement that
startles the crowd; an extraordinary matter is undeniably an
extraordinary matter. Great Master Yunmen could be said to
have been strong and stern for a time. You should avoid bit-
ing in here.

TRANSLATOR'S COMMENTS

The figure of the great master Yunmen has already been seen in koans number fifteen and sixteen in this collection, "Threescore Blows" and "Putting on a Formal Vestment at the Sound of a Bell," both of which deal with the manifest world. The koan at hand also deals with the manifest world, and is of the same kind as number eighteen, "Three Pounds," which featured Yunmen's disciple Dongshan.

Wumen's prose commentary is typically artful. "When the house is poor" means when you come to realize the poverty of thought and language in comparison to the richness of the direct experience of suchness. In metaphysical terms, "poverty" here symbolizes the transcendental nature of absolute reality as it is in itself.

In either sense Wumen can say of Yunmen that "it is hard to get even a simple meal together." Wumen seemingly chides Yunmen for his crude reply, but is actually affirming the impossibility of accurately depicting absolute reality in any relative terms.

Turning his attention to the other side of the coin, the infinity of the suchness of being-as-is, to which Yunmen summarily points with a "dry turd," Wumen makes the wry remark, "When things are busy, there's no time to write." Here, the expression "things are busy" refers to the infinity of suchness, which is endless in both complexity and extent. "There's no time to write" means that it is impossible to describe this infinity in words; so Yunmen simply notes something near at hand to represent what is everywhere.

One sense of Wumen's remarks is to reemphasize the point, made again and again in Zen comments on koans, that the use of a specific object is not meant literally.

Wumen's verse comment stresses the immediacy of direct perception, faster even than thought.

The comment of Zen master Li-an (pronounced Lee-ahn) is extremely useful. He begins by explaining the use of the turd to shock people out of routine thinking. The "strength" and "sternness" of great master Yunmen that Li-an praises refer to the inadmissibility of any subjective ideas or judgments in regard to Yunmen's meaning. Zen master Li-an concludes his remarks by telling the reader to "avoid biting in" to this dry turd, meaning as usual that a superficial concern with the literal meaning of Yunmen's symbolic reply is an irrelevant distraction best avoided.

This sort of reminder still applies today. Most translators mistranslate this koan to start with, and then purport to explain the koan by superficial concern with the literal meaning of the mistranslation. This is not an ancient Zen toilet joke; even on the level of ordinary logic, its reference is elsewhere.

As far as the manifest content is concerned, Yunmen's reply alludes to a story in the Taoist classic *Chuang-tzu* involving a series of questions and answers regarding the whereabouts of the Tao, or natural law. The Taoist master acknowledges the omnipresence of the Tao, even in an object so lowly as a piece of dung.

Yunmen and some of his major disciples were known for their astounding ability to pull a line from the ocean of Chinese literature to reply to questions about Zen psychology. Although this technique requires use of the intellect, it is not and cannot be done solely by the intellect, which acts as an instrument and is not in itself the operator.

Yunmen's baffling skills in getting his mind to work on several levels of meaning with lightninglike speed reflect something of the liberation of complete Zen mastery. His sayings are often so cryptic on the surface that fakery is easy with an unsophisticated audience.

The best way to see through this is to understand all the

levels at which Yunmen (or any other Zen master) simultaneously spoke. Then avoid people who are as incoherent below the surface as they are mysterious on the surface. Zen is not a game of riddles and quips, but there have always been people who make it out to be that way. "Yunmen's Turd" is a good testing koan, to see who can tell the difference between Buddhism and a pile of crap.

22

Kashyapa's Flagpole

Ananda asked Kashyapa, "Aside from the golden-sleeved robe, what did the Buddha hand on to you?"

Kashyapa called, "Ananda!"

Ananda responded, "Yes?"

Kashyapa said, "Take down the flagpole in front of the gate."

WUMEN SAYS,

If you can utter a pivotal saying here, you will personally see the congregation on Spiritual Mountain, still there intact. Otherwise, "An ancient Buddha focused on it from the start, yet still hasn't found the marvel yet."

WUMEN'S VERSE

How was the point of the question as intimate as the point of the answer?

How many people have developed muscles in their eyes from this?

Elder brother calls, younger brother responds, bringing out the family disgrace;

Not in the province of dark and light, this is a special springtime.

TRANSLATOR'S COMMENTS

Kashyapa has already been seen in the sixth case, "Buddha Picks Up a Flower." He was one of Gautama Buddha's main apprentices, and Zen Buddhists consider him the first master after Buddha in the transmission of Zen. According to the *Scripture of the Great Extinction,* one of the major texts of Buddhism, this Kashyapa was the only disciple not present at the death of the Buddha. In esoteric tradition this is interpreted to mean that he was truly independent and equal to the Buddha, through having realized the living truth that the Buddha realized.

According to Zen legend, Kashyapa was singled out as the Buddha's successor, represented by his inheritance of Buddha's golden-sleeved robe. When Ananda, another disciple, asked Kashyapa about the inner transmission symbolized by the outward succession, Kashyapa called him by name, using an outward representation to hint at an inner reality, the essence of the mind that asks and answers.

In ancient India, where this dialogue is supposed to have taken place, debates were signaled by hoisting a flag at the gate of the sanctuary. Having pointed to Ananda's own mind, Kashyapa tells him to take down the flagpole, signifying that there is no debate between them in the sense that the original Buddha-mind is equal in all people.

Wumen's prose comment follows up on this sense of the omnipresence of the Buddha-mind. Spiritual Mountain is a famous site of Buddha's teaching, already met with in the sixth koan. Naturally, it represents suchness, the context of enlightenment. Wumen says you will see the congregation still there when you understand this story, in the sense of realizing the inner essence of awakening that is one and the same in all times and places. If you don't understand, he says, then cast your eyes on infinity beyond all possible knowledge; this will "take your flagpole down."

Wumen's verse begins by using the icons of these two disciples of Buddha to contrast form (represented by Ananda) with essence (represented by Kashyapa). He then goes on to recommend the exercise of this discernment. Summing up the action, Wumen says, "Elder brother calls, younger brother responds." Ananda is considered the spiritual successor of Kashyapa; their interaction in this koan represents the activity of Zen teachership, which "brings out the family disgrace," a typically ironic way of speaking about enlightenment.

Enlightenment is called the family disgrace in two senses. One implication is that awakening is needed precisely because of degeneration in human consciousness, so recognition of the need for enlightenment can be called bringing out the disgrace of the family of humankind.

The other implication of enlightenment bringing out the family disgrace is that Zen masters traditionally do not claim enlightenment. This attitude is not adopted out of professional humility, but because they actually do realize the infinity of reality.

Wumen concludes with a beautiful description of the experience and life of enlightenment, beyond the fluctuation of human thoughts of affirmation and denial.

Many comments by other Zen masters illustrate various aspects of this important koan. Zen master Fenyang, who was one of the pioneers of Zen koan training, said, ostensibly of Ananda, "How would he know if he didn't ask?" This means that even though Buddha-nature is the very essence of mind and therefore everpresent, nevertheless attention and effort is needed to bring it into consciousness.

Zen master Yunju used this koan to refer to two basic issues of Zen: "If you understand before the flagpole is taken down, you bury the ancient religion; if you understand after the flagpole is taken down, you let yourself down." This means that if you cling to outward forms as sacred in themselves, you obscure the eternal source of conscious being itself; but if you cling to annihilation of forms as truth, you deny your own life in the world.

Zen master Lingyuan remarked, "Everyone says that Kashyapa only knew how to dismantle, not how to reconstruct. What they do not realize is that he put a toxic drug in the milk that can kill people and can also enliven them, causing the twenty-eight Indian and six Chinese patriarchs of Zen to break their bones and split their skin, such that the blood drips on the road of Zen to this very day."

What this comment means to say is that the figure of Kashyapa in this koan is usually interpreted to stand for the heart of nirvana, referring specifically to his image of "taking down the flagpole." Lingyuan points out that this is a partial understanding, one that overlooks his call to Ananda, which was both a call to the essence of mind and a gesture of pointing to being-as-is.

This is the "toxic drug in the milk" that can both kill and enliven. It kills those who identify their own subjective minds with Buddha-nature, enlivens those who have attained nirvana and clarified their perceptions.

When Lingyuan says the Zen patriarchs "broke their bones and split their skin, such that the blood drips on the road of Zen to this very day," he means that they practiced the transcendence realized in nirvana as well as the compassion realized in being-as-is, devoting this completeness of spiritual development to the edification of others.

23

Not Thinking of Good or Evil

The Sixth Patriarch of Zen was pursued by Elder Ming all the way to a mountain ridge. When the Patriarch saw Ming coming, he cast the robe and bowl [of the patriarchate] onto a rock and said, "This robe symbolizes faith; could it be right to fight over it? You can take it away."

Ming tried to pick it up, but it was immovable as a mountain. Vacillating, in fear, Ming said, "I have come for the Teaching, not the robe. Please instruct me."

The Patriarch said, "Not thinking good, not thinking evil, right at this very moment, what is your original face?"

Ming immediately attained great enlightenment. His whole body ran with sweat. In tears, he bowed and asked, "Is there any meaning beyond the esoteric intent of the esoteric words you have just spoken?"

The Patriarch said, "What I have just told you is not esoteric. If you turn your attention around to your own state, the secret is after all in you."

Ming said, "Though I went along with the assembly at Huangmei, in reality I had not seen into my own state. Now that you have pointed out a way of entry, I am like a person who drinks water and knows for himself whether it is warm or cool. Now you are my teacher."

The Patriarch said, "If you are thus, then you and I alike are students of the Fifth Patriarch. Keep it well on your own."

WUMEN SAYS,

Of the Sixth Patriarch it could be said, "The matter comes from a busy house." He was so kind that it was as if he had peeled a fresh lychee, removed the seed, and put it in your mouth, so all you have to do is swallow.

WUMEN'S VERSE

It cannot be depicted, cannot be drawn;
It cannot be praised enough, stop trying to sense it.
The original face has nowhere to hide—
When the world disintegrates, this does not decay.

ZEN MASTER FENYANG'S VERSE

Few people believe in the Buddha in their own mind;
Unwilling to take responsibility for it, they suffer a lot of
* cramps.*
Arbitrary ideas, greed and anger, the wrappings of
* afflictions,*
All are conditioned on attachment to the cave of ignorance.

TRANSLATOR'S COMMENTS

The Sixth Patriarch of Zen was the last in a line of early masters who established Zen in China. The figure of the

Sixth Patriarch is one of the most important icons in Zen lore, representing the universality of Zen.

Before his enlightenment, the Sixth Patriarch had been an illiterate woodcutter from a frontier area. As a young man, he was suddenly awakened to the truth of Zen one day when he happened to hear a line of a Buddhist scripture being recited in the streets of the marketplace where he sold his wood.

After this experience, the young woodcutter went to see the Buddhist master of the age, who at that time (in the seventh century) was the Fifth Patriarch of Zen.

The new illuminate found the Fifth Patriarch at a place called Huangmei (pronounced Hwong-may), near the ancient heartlands of Chinese culture, surrounded by seven hundred of the most educated and intelligent clerics of the day.

The young woodcutter from the boondocks could not read classical Chinese or speak a cultivated dialect, but the Fifth Patriarch recognized the light of enlightenment in his simple genuineness. The story of the first encounter between these two is traditionally used as a symbol of the principle that the Buddha-nature in the essence of mind transcends all ethnic and cultural difference, being inherently universal to humankind and not acquired by specialized history or conditioning.

Fearing the jealousy of the monks surrounding him, the Fifth Patriarch sent the enlightened young woodcutter to work in the mill of the teaching center. Since there were as many as seven hundred students at the monastery of Huangmei, there were also a large number of workers who were not clerics, but helped with the upkeep of the grounds and infrastructure of the Buddhist community. This pious tradition began in India and has continued in all countries where Buddhism has had public institutions. It was among these workers that the fledgling Sixth Patriarch was first hidden from the jealousy of the learned clerics, who naturally represent intellectual snobbery in the symbolic historiography of Zen.

Not long after that, the Fifth Patriarch retired. Everyone wanted to know who the sixth patriarch was going to be. He told them it was that illiterate woodcutter from the frontier who had been working in the mill for the last few months. When they went to look for him, the enraged clerics and scholars found that he had disappeared.

In the story underlying the koan at hand, Elder Ming was the leader of a group of those who pursued the new Sixth Patriarch in high dudgeon. History says Elder Ming had actually been a military commander before retiring into Buddhist orders; thus he is a perfect icon for this role in this koan, which is to represent aggression as an outgrowth of arrogance and presumption.

When Ming caught up with him, the Sixth Patriarch willingly handed over the robe of the patriarchate, popularly believed to be the same robe that Buddha handed to Kashyapa. The symbolic meaning of this act is that what is essential is the heart of the teaching, not its outer dressing. If the formalities of Buddhism had become objects of ambition and contention, the Sixth Patriarch was certainly willing to give them up in order to preserve the living heart; more than willing, he was obliged.

As it turned out, Ming could not even lift the robe. The living meaning of Buddhism cannot be understood on demand, or by insisting on picking it up by preconceived ideas. Even the formalities of Buddhist practices cannot be wielded with genuine effect by those who are really just ambitious self-seekers underneath it all.

Suddenly Ming had a change of heart. He realized that what he really needed was truth, not the mere name or claim of truth. This is also a representation of the universality of Buddha-nature in all conscious beings. Even an egotistic, compulsive, and tyrannical mentality has an opportunity to change its orientation and act through original Buddha-nature rather than through the personality of conditioned mental habits.

Then the Sixth Patriarch taught Ming an exercise in Zen introspection: "Not thinking good, not thinking evil, right at this very moment, what is your original face?" In Zen, introspection does not mean looking into your inward thoughts and feelings; it means looking into the source and essence of consciousness. "Thinking good and evil" means continuously thinking about one thing or another, and then reacting to your own thoughts emotionally and intellectually, learning to represent artificial conceptions and opinions to yourself as objective truths. In order to introspect in the Zen sense, this process of "thinking good and evil," and its preoccupation with mental contents, are suspended for the sake of clarity of vision into the impersonal essence of mind underlying all consciousness.

In Wumen's prose comment, he praises the Sixth Patriarch for presenting such a simple method of realization. Just as Wumen often makes a hidden point underlying a surface of apparent criticism or sarcasm, here he also issues a traditional warning under the surface of what looks like praise. As Wumen hints from the start, the method set forth here by the Sixth Patriarch is just an expedient, designed to cut directly through the tangle of confused thinking; one should not let its simplicity mislead one into a halfhearted or simplistic approach to the exercise.

The verse of Zen master Fenyang, who, it will be remembered, was one of the founders of Zen koan study, also emphasizes the purely practical aspect of the method taught by the Sixth Patriarch. When he says, "Few people believe in the Buddha in their own mind," he is not referring to religious faith as ordinarily conceived, but to the pragmatic fact that the experience of Buddha-nature is not an idea or a thought, and is therefore unfamiliar to the ordinary thinking mind.

"Unwilling to take responsibility for it," Fenyang goes

on, referring to inability to avail ourselves of the Buddha-nature within because of compulsive habits of thought that obscure it, "they suffer a lot of cramps." People who are alienated from Buddha-nature and therefore restricted by their preconditioned mentalities and habits of thought cannot experience the freedom of Buddhahood.

Finally, Fenyang gives the traditional diagnosis of this problem, which also indicates what the patient should avoid during the course of treatment: "Arbitrary ideas, greed and anger, the wrappings of afflictions." This is a more elaborate way of describing what the Sixth Patriarch called "thinking good and thinking evil," which can be transcended for the very fact that it is not ultimate objective reality itself, but "conditioned on attachment to the cave of ignorance." To see the "original face" of the essential mind we need to stop thinking about our own imaginings, and find "the secret in ourselves."

24

Detachment from Words

Master Fengxue was asked by a monk, " 'Speech and silence involve alienation and vagueness'—how does one get through without transgression?"

Fengxue said, "I always remember South of the Lake in springtime, the hundred flowers fragrant where the partridges call."

WUMEN SAYS,

Fengxue's mind is like lightning; finding a road, he immediately goes on it. Nevertheless, he did not entirely cut off the tongue of the ancient quoted. If you can see intimately here, you will have your own way of expression.

But try to make a statement apart from absorption in words.

WUMEN'S VERSE

He doesn't reveal a stylish phrase;
It's already imparted before speaking.
If you step forward chattering,
I know you are really at a loss.

ZEN MASTER ZHONGFENG SAID,
This monk's question was like a flood reaching the sky, engulfing everything in its waves. Fengxue could certainly go into water without drowning, but how could he do anything about being completely immersed?

ZEN MASTER DAHUI'S VERSE
Suddenly going out the gate, first he sees the road;
As soon as he sets down his foot, he climbs into a boat.
The secret of spiritual immortals is truly worth preserving—
Even parent-child intimacy does not make transmission
*   possible.*

ZEN MASTER FOJIAN'S VERSE
In the shadows of the colored clouds, a spiritual immortal
*   appears;*
In his hand he holds a fan of scarlet gauze, screening his
*   face.*
It is urgently necessary to set your eyes on the immortal;
Don't gaze at the fan in the immortal's hand.

TRANSLATOR'S COMMENTS

Zen master Fengxue (pronounced Fung-shweh) lived in the tenth century. An exceptionally brilliant master, Fengxue was one of the very last teachers of the original Linji school of Zen in his time. It was only through the work of his spiritual descendants that the ego-shattering impact of Linji Zen was preserved and transmitted to future generations. It was also through the combination of spirituality and intelligence in Fengxue and his school that Linji Zen was able to absorb the methods of other Zen schools and use them effectively even after the disappearance of the parent traditions.

The question in the koan at hand makes reference to a pre-Zen Chinese Buddhist classic, probably the first native Chinese Buddhist work all about absolute reality as it is in itself. This was highly admired by Zen Buddhists. As someone noted for unusual development of both intelligence and insight, Fengxue is well suited to be the master icon in this story, to answer a subtle question about the ultimate truth.

The issue in the koan at hand is this: "Speech," which also means ratiocinative thinking, involves alienation from inconceivable ultimate truth, while "silence," which also means unthinking, involves vagueness about what may or may not be implied or discerned. The question is how to relate to reality without falling into either extreme. The essential point is to transcend habitual thinking without compromising precise awareness.

Here, Zen master Fengxue responds with a little bit of scenery, which as often seen in Zen lore symbolizes the direct experience of being-as-is or suchness. In its infinity, suchness is beyond speech and thought; yet the experience of suchness cannot be a dead silence, because it contains everything.

At first, Wumen's prose comment looks like praise of Fengxue. As usual, it is really a technical description of the action, in this case direct perception of suchness. Then Wumen seems to qualify his praise, saying, "Nevertheless, he did not entirely cut off the tongue of the ancient quoted," meaning that it is still important, for practical purposes, to contemplate the original question. Only by your own experience, in Wumen's words "seeing intimately," can you "have your own way of expression." As usual, Wumen concludes by urging the reader to proceed from intellectual understanding ("absorption in words") to actual application.

Wumen's verse comment underscores the point that the

real answer is in the direct experience of reality, not in clever talk. "It's already imparted before speaking" because reality is already there. So "if you step forward chattering," just paying attention to words and images, "I know you are really at a loss."

The comments of the other Zen masters cited also emphasize the practical aspect of dealing with this koan. Zhongfeng affirms that the seeker's question, which really represents concentration technique, applies to the total field of awareness and experience, and thus should be practiced in the context of all activities.

Then he goes on to describe Fengxue's answer, which really represents the effect of the technique, absorption in suchness, and concludes with a warning to avoid being so captivated by the forms and colors of suchness that the heart of nirvana is lost.

The verse of Zen master Dahui begins with a description of the immediacy of suchness, and ends with a reminder that this can only be understood in its real sense at first hand. Thus he says, "Even parent-child intimacy does not make transmission possible," meaning that reality directly experienced is your own realization and cannot be obtained from another or communicated to another as it is in itself.

Finally, the verse of Zen master Fojian presents a colorful description of the koan, not as a display of literary skill to match the sophistication of this story, but as a warning to avoid being diverted by the verbal expression, or even by the sensual experience: In order to see the point of the Zen master's indirect answer, he says, "Set your eyes on the immortal; / Don't gaze at the fan in the immortal's hand." The aim is the "immortal," the essence of mind that is able to contact reality without alienation or vagueness, not "the fan in the immortal's hand," the scene conjured up to announce the immortal's presence.

 **25**

Sermon from the Third Seat

Master Yangshan dreamed that he went to where the future Buddha Maitreya was, and was assigned to the third seat.

Then one of the saints there struck a gavel and said, "Today it is the turn of the one in the third seat to preach."

So Yangshan got up, struck the gavel, and said, "The teaching of the universal vehicle is beyond all propositions and denials. Listen clearly!"

WUMEN SAYS,

Tell me, was this preaching or not? Open your mouth and you miss; but keep your mouth closed and you lose. If you neither open nor shut it—108,000.

WUMEN'S VERSE

In the bright sunlight on a clear day
He speaks of a dream in a dream.
Making up wonders,
He fools the whole crowd.

TRANSLATOR'S COMMENTS

Yangshan (pronounced Yahng-shahn) was one of the greatest of the classical Zen teachers. He lived in the ninth century and studied with several of the ancient masters. Renowned for both spiritual and intellectual brilliance, Yangshan had many distinguished disciples and was said to have attracted seekers from as far away as India and Central Asia. He and his teacher Guishan (pronounced Gway-shahn), who appears in a later koan, were among the very first Zen masters to construct koans deliberately, long before koans became a routine part of Zen training.

In the koan at hand, Yangshan relates a dream in which he went to the heaven where the future Buddha lives. In traditional Buddhist lore, the future Buddha who is to succeed Gautama Buddha and usher in a new era is called Maitreya, whose name means "The Loving One" or "The Kindly One." The abode of future Buddhas, furthermore, is a heavenly state called Tushita (pronounced Too-shee-tuh), which means "Satisfied" and "Happy."

Asked to give a lecture on the occasion of his dream visit to this heaven, Yangshan got up, called everyone to attention, and stated the timeless liberative teaching of Buddhism that universal absolute truth is beyond all categories of human thought. Then he closed by once again calling forth presence of mind.

Wumen poses the question, was this preaching or not? Before we can answer, he warns us that neither speech nor silence can express it. The Buddhist philosopher Nagarjuna (pronounced Naa-gaar-joo-nah), who was also a Zen patriarch, wrote about this pivotal issue in these terms: "Without relying on conventional usage, absolute truth cannot be expressed; without going to ultimate truth, nirvana cannot be attained."

Thus it is necessary to make use of structure, including language, in order to formulate ways of approaching ultimate truth; but it is essential to avoid being mesmerized thereby into taking those structures themselves for ultimate truth. The traditional mental posture of universalistic Buddhist practice is therefore described as "neither grasping nor rejecting." Nirvana is realized by "not grasping," suchness is experienced by "not rejecting."

Wumen concludes his prose comment, which is simply a mirror of the exercise Yangshan presented to the denizens of the state of contentment, with another warning about suchness, reminding us not to understand it vaguely and subconsciously identify it with subjective ideas: "If you neither open nor shut" your mouth, he says, meaning that if you do not have an articulate awareness and yet are not unconscious, "108,000."

"One hundred and eight thousand" what? If you go for the "what?" you will surely find at least that many possibilities. "108,000" is a symbolic number representing all the feelings, thoughts, and ideas that can come between you and objective reality.

On the brighter side, of course, Wumen's comment can also be read to mean that if you avoid the extremes of attachment and rejection, there are an infinite number of possibilities of perception, experience, appreciation, and understanding available to the liberated mind.

Wumen's verse begins by affirming Yangshan's message that ultimate reality is omnipresent, like the sunlight on a clear day. This is contrasted to the "dream in a dream," which is the conceptualized version of reality constructed by the thought habits of the subjective mind, or what Yangshan referred to as "all propositions and denials."

In the third line of Wumen's verse, "making up wonders" may be used to expose the objective unreality of subjective ideas; and it may be used to express wonder at what Buddhist scripture calls the "magic of knowledge." The magic of knowledge is the capacity of the mind to apprehend a total field of experience as one unified reality, and also to handle order, structure, and logic with full awareness of the "magical" nature of mental construction.

When Wumen says in the end that Yangshan's scenario "fools the whole crowd," he again warns us not to be captivated by the outward appearance of this exercise when focusing on the mental posture of balance that it is designed to foster.

As usual, at the same time and in the same words Wumen indirectly makes a metaphysical statement about the nature of "knowledge." Being in the conventional sense a matter of consensus by definition, in comparison to absolute truth it is as subjective as a dream.

This statement and this realization have an unsuspected depth of intricacy, and no one should expect to understand them at one reading or at first thought. While you try to understand the structure of this meditation, cut through any confusing thoughts that arise by asking yourself, "Who dreams the dreamer of the dream?"

The verse of Zen master Benjiao (pronounced Bun-jiao) tells us that when we practice and realize this teaching of Buddha, there is no need for any special mention of it, because our direct experience of everything is a reminder of its truth and living reality. Thus it is best to practice and realize it in the midst of everything, without telling yourself you are doing so at all.

But if you get to feeling self-satisfied along the way, you can find out if you are still awake by observing your reaction to the crack of the Zen gavel.

26

Two Monks Roll up a Screen

Master Fayan came up for consultation before the communal meal. He pointed to a bamboo screen, and two monks then both went to roll it up. Fayan said, "One gain, one loss."

WUMEN SAYS,
Tell me, whose gain is it, whose loss? If you can focus a single eye here, you will know where the master failed. Even so, it is of utmost importance to avoid discussing this in terms of gain and loss.

WUMEN'S VERSE
Rolling up, there's utter clarity, penetrating space;
But even space does not accord with our source.
Better to let go of everything, from space on,
For such subtle secrecy that nothing can get in.

TRANSLATOR'S COMMENTS

Fayan (pronounced Fah-yen) was one of the great classical masters. He was born in the late ninth century and lived well into the tenth century. Among his numerous enlightened disciples were four National Teachers of Chinese and Korean kingdoms. As a figure in Zen iconography, Fayan is noted for subtle dialectic.

The koan at hand is a story of a test, much like koan number eleven, "Testing Hermits." Later the story of the test came to be employed as a test itself, by virtue of its capacity for producing doubt in the mind. Many people imagine that the Zen master was saying one monk was right and one was wrong, then puzzle over the apparent conundrum of which was which: *This* is "one loss." Some people see the Zen master's test: *This* is "one gain."

Also, when anything is taken up, something else is left aside: This too is "one gain, one loss." The point of the Zen exercise using this perspective is not to seek gain and avoid loss per se, but to note the working of "one gain, one loss" in what you do and what goes on around you. This is a way to enlarge your perspective on events and make the most of the power of choice.

In Wumen's prose comment, he immediately indicates that the function of this koan is testing and doubt-producing. When you see the whole perspective, he continues, you will know "where the master failed," in the sense that you will see the ambiguity that looks like partiality or arbitrary discrimination. Finally Wumen reveals the secret of this koan, saying "it is of utmost importance to avoid discussing this in terms of gain and loss."

In his verse comment, Wumen speaks of the absolute: "Rolling up" seems to refer to the rolling up of the blind, but it actually stands for putting away all conjecture and speculation. This produces a state of "utter clarity, penetrating space," which might be called viewing true suchness with the eye of nirvana.

Typically, Wumen goes on to discuss the limitation of this exercise when pursued alone to the exclusion of knowledge of differentiation, cautioning the buoyant practitioner of spacelike consciousness that "even space does not accord with our source." This has two meanings. One is that the heart of nirvana does not mean being "spaced out," or empty-headed. The second is that nirvana alone is not the source of reality, it is the way to the source. The first level of warning is for errant practitioners; the second is for genuine practitioners.

In the third line Wumen describes what Buddhists called the "emptiness of emptiness," which you realize when you "let go of everything *from space on.*" This means that you begin by the exercise of a mind like space, containing the whole universe yet in essence not fixed or obstructed anywhere, then progress from this level of detachment to a more advanced level that includes detachment from detachment itself. This is the state when samsara and nirvana are united so perfectly that the distinction between them is a matter of "such subtle secrecy that nothing can get in."

The comments of other Zen masters also reinforce the sense of this koan as a testing instrument, and also tell how to look at the story.

Zen master Huanglong (pronounced Hwong-loong) said, "Fayan had a sharp sword in his hand, killing and giving life according to the time. Both monks went at the same time to roll up the screen: Tell me, which one gained and which one lost? Do you understand? For mundane affairs, just use impartiality to decide them; the human mind can hardly be made equal to the disk of the moon."

Huanglong's final remark means that vision of absolute reality is not obtained through human discrimination.

Zen master Nanjian (pronounced Nahn-jyen) remarked, "Fayan was probing, the two monks were chasing a clod. Even if the wrap-up was quick, there was still no avoiding biting the dust on level ground."

The expression "chasing a clod" likens delusion to a dog that is hit with a clod of earth thrown by a man, then angrily chases the clod instead of the man. The image is of the human mind becoming captivated, deceived, and even tormented by its own thoughts and constructions, never turning attention to the ultimate source of thought itself. The final remark that there is no avoiding "biting the dust on level ground" refers to the human proneness to automatic thinking that this koan exposes.

Zen master Caoqi (pronounced Tsao-chee) reinforced these observations when he said, "Old Fayan sure had a magic spearhead on the tip of his finger! The two monks didn't manage to dodge it, and couldn't avoid losing their lives. If they had been of the right stuff, they'd have flipped over his chair the minute he pointed at the screen." The magic spearhead is the testing function of his action. The "two monks" who didn't manage to dodge it are those who think in terms of either/or, gain and loss. Those with the "right stuff" of genuine insight and complete perspective, in contrast, see that what looks like a question is in fact an answer, thus turning the test into a lesson, and thereby "flipping over" the pivotal basis of understanding.

One of the greatest tests in Zen koan study is the fact that so much Zen literature contains coherent but superficial meanings as well as coherent and profound meanings. By understanding people's understanding, it is thereby possible to discern whether they are shallow in their perceptions or whether they see below the surface. Yet an observer may also understand understanding either superficially or deeply. That is why remembering the principle of "one gain, one loss" helps us wake up completely.

27

It Is Not Mind or Buddha

A monk asked Master Nanquan, "Is there a truth not spoken to people?"

Nanquan said, "There is."

The monk asked, "What is the truth not spoken to people?"

Nanquan said, "It is not mind, it is not Buddha, it is not a thing."

WUMEN SAYS,

Confronted with this question, Nanquan could only put forth all he had; he was quite a dotard.

WUMEN'S VERSE

Meticulous instruction diminishes your virtue;
The unspoken truly has effect.
Even if the oceans transmute,
It's never conveyed to you.

TRANSLATOR'S COMMENTS

Nanquan was the great early classical master met with in koan number fourteen, "Killing a Cat," and koan number nineteen, "The Normal Is the Way." It may be useful to recall here that Nanquan's main function as an icon in Zen lore is to remind seekers that absolute reality in itself transcends any conception we may form of it.

The present koan is also of this nature. According to Zen Buddhist understanding, there is no way to actually describe the direct experience of reality as such; you can only realize it for yourself. This is metaphorically described as a "taboo name," the ultimate reality that can only be witnessed and cannot be spoken.

In practical terms, Nanquan's answer describes a three-part exercise in detachment. It should be remembered, of course, that in Buddhism the practice and experience of detachment do not mean rejection or destruction of that from which one detaches. With that understood, the process Nanquan depicts is clear. "It is not mind" refers to the stage of detachment from thoughts, "it is not Buddha" refers to the stage of detachment from clear consciousness; "it is not a thing" refers to the stage of detachment from immediate perception.

What lies beyond this procedure is the experience that cannot be spoken. In both his prose and verse comments, Wumen's extreme reserve further underscores the point that this process is something one works through, not something that yields meaning to theoretical discussion.

In his prose remark Wumen says Nanquan "put forth all he had," indicating that this roundabout reference to the "unspoken truth" encompasses the full range of initiatory practice.

In his verse Wumen deliberately stresses the idea that the unspoken and unexpressed in Nanquan's answer cannot be filled in by words. This is the usual invitation to see for ourselves.

28

Long Have I Heard

Once Deshan questioned Master Longtan until late at night. Longtan said, "It is late; why don't you retire?"

So Deshan said good-bye and raised the screen to go. Seeing that it was pitch dark outside, he turned around and said, "It's dark outside."

So Longtan lit a paper torch and handed it to Deshan. As Deshan reached out to take the lamp, Longtan blew it out.

At this Deshan suddenly had an insight. He bowed to Longtan, who asked him, "What principle have you seen?"

Deshan said, "From now on I won't doubt the utterances of the Zen masters."

The next day Longtan went up in the hall and said, "There is someone here whose fangs are like sword trees, whose mouth is like a bowl of blood. Even if you hit him with a stick he won't turn his head. Some day he will establish our Way on the summit of a solitary peak."

Deshan subsequently placed his commentaries in front of the teaching hall, took up a torch, and said, "Even to investigate all the mystic discernments is like a hair tossed into space; even to exhaust the pivotal workings of the world is like a drop thrown into a gigantic canyon." Then he burned his commentaries, bowed, and left.

WUMEN SAYS,

Before he left northern China, Deshan was in a state of high dudgeon; he made his way South, determined to destroy the teaching of a special transmission outside of doctrine.

On the road, Deshan asked a woman if he could buy some refreshments from her. She said, "What writings are you carrying in your knapsack, O Worthy?"

Deshan replied that they were commentaries on the Diamond Cutter Scripture.

The woman said, "How about where it says in that scripture, 'Past mind cannot be grasped, present mind cannot be grasped, future mind cannot be grasped'—which mind do you want to refresh, O Worthy?"

Faced with this question, Deshan could only frown. But even so, he did not die at the woman's words; he asked her if there were any Zen teachers around. The woman said there was a master Longtan a couple of miles away.

When he got to Longtan, Deshan experienced complete defeat. It could be said that his earlier words did not match his later talk.

As for Longtan, he very much seems to have been unconscious of being unseemly, because of his compassion for a child. Seeing the other had some live embers in him, Longtan hurriedly took some foul water and doused him, putting the fire out. When you look, it's a laughable scene.

WUMEN'S VERSE

Hearing the name is not like seeing the face,
Seeing the face is not like hearing the name.
Even though he managed to save his nostrils,
Nonetheless he blinded his eyes.

ZEN MASTER BAIYUN'S VERSE

When light and dark overcome each other, that is not
*   worth talking about;*
As long as there is any interpretation, this is not yet
*   intimacy.*
When the paper torch went out, the eyes emerged,
Breaking through the empire of China, finding no one at
*   all.*

ZEN MASTER BAONING'S VERSE

All at once a cascade comes down before the cliff;
In the middle of the night, the sun is bright in the palm of
*   his hand.*
Opening wide his mouth, he expresses the energy of spirit;
With whom will he travel freely throughout the world?

ZEN MASTER DAHONG'S VERSE

When light and dark form each other, things are vague
*   and remote;*
Who would have known the back of his head would gush
*   with spiritual light?*
All in all he drew the line, cutting off the path of a
*   thousand distinctions;*
South, North, East, West, he arrives at his native village.

TRANSLATOR'S COMMENTS

Deshan has already been seen in koan number thirteen, "Deshan Carrying His Bowl." Longtan (pronounced Loong-tahn) was his Zen teacher, otherwise little known. Like Nanquan, Deshan's iconographical function in Zen lore is mostly quite specialized.

The koan at hand, which purports to represent Deshan's Zen awakening, is a good example of the symbolism of the figure of Deshan in Zen koan literature. Overall, the story illustrates a sudden shift from ratiocinative conceptual consciousness to immediate all-at-once cosmic consciousness.

In the main recital, the "darkness outside" represents unknown dimensions of reality beyond the confines of ordinary perception and thought. The Zen teacher hands the hesitant seeker a paper torch, which represents the ordinary exercise of the intellect, thus demonstrating the incommensurability of the tiny light of the torch with the immense vastness of the dark. This simple action further shows how the impression of illumination given off by the torch depends on keeping the eyes trained on the immediate vicinity of the torch itself, just as reason only works within its own self-circumscribed parameters.

Having absorbed the seeker in this overwhelming realization, the teacher suddenly extinguishes the little "light" of conceptual thought, all at once letting the rest of Deshan's mind sense the immense "dark" of the unknown infinite. To borrow some of the images of Zen master Baiyun (pronounced Bye-ywun) and Zen master Dahong (pronounced Dah-hoong), this symbolizes the experience of nirvana and the awakening of "spiritual light," a level of consciousness that is more fundamental and more subtle than the contrasting "light" and "dark" of formal knowledge and ignorance.

At the end of the main recital, the newly awakened Deshan burns his books, which were in fact books about books about some of the ways of getting to reality. This means that he no longer used them for the purposes of academic discussion or philosophical speculation, but digested them in the fire of direct experience. Deshan's own words on the occasion are often quoted in later Zen lore to describe the contrast between the experiences of ordinary thinking and academic intellectual exercise on the one hand and the experience of direct perception of reality on the other. Notice that all of the verses of the Zen masters also talk about this.

Longtan himself, the ancient master of the koan, also eulogizes Deshan in terms suggestive of nirvana, with images of fangs, a bowl of blood, indifference, and solitariness, all of which evoke the image of esoteric death. Zen Taoists refer to this as death of the human mentality in order that the immortal spirit may live.

Wumen's long prose comment gives some background to this koan, which should as usual be understood in a pragmatic sense rather than a literary or folkloric sense.

Northern China was the ancient seat of Chinese civilization, and represents conformity and rigidity. The South, in contrast, means the process and destination of Buddhism, which is liberation. Deshan himself was a Buddhist scholar who was very much attached to formal learning, and very much attached to the feeling of being one of those who enjoyed this dignity.

Buddhist scholars have often had a problem with Zen masters, because the scholars specialized in formal exegesis of particular texts and doctrines, while the Zen masters were not attached to any school of dogma. This is why the scholar Deshan was in "high dudgeon" and desirous of destroying the Zen teaching of a "special transmission outside of doctrine" through direct experience. This schism was something like the Churchmen versus the Gnostics in terms of Christian history.

Deshan the scholar was stopped in his tracks by a woman selling tea and cakes by the roadside. As it happens, this was an enlightened individual, many of whom were known to set up roadside stalls such as this in order to support themselves and also to contact the people, both Zen seekers and ordinary folk, who passed by that way. Naturally, many such people lived in the areas of China where numerous genuine Zen masters were active.

The woman in this story could see Deshan's condition, so she set a trap for him, using the very book that he studied, a popular text known as the *Diamond Cutter Scripture*, which is in one sense all about nonattachment to form. As a matter of fact, the Sixth Patriarch of Zen, who was seen in koan number twenty-three, "Not Thinking of Good or Evil," first awakened on hearing a single line from this scripture: "You should enliven the mind without dwelling on anything."

By the way, notice that while the text Deshan studied was well known, the woman did not necessarily know what it was when she started to set her trap. There were actually many possibilities, including some very arcane and difficult treatises studied by many scholarly clerics. But leaving aside chance and prescience, we can also say she wasn't being either foolhardy or bold: One of the marks of genuine Zen adepts is that they can actually interpret any authentic Buddhist system coherently, even if they have never studied it formally.

There have been several masters in history especially noted for their remarkable talents in this area, but the ability is very widespread in records of real Zen Buddhists of the past. Of course, many Zen masters cultivated this ability through firsthand study of Buddhist doctrines and schools, either deliberately or as a matter of course. In ancient China, however, laywomen were not usually supposed or allowed to obtain as much formal education as men, so for the purposes of symbolic iconography the woman in this story represents essential understanding as contrasted to acquired knowledge.

As for the portion of scripture cited by the woman, see how the question she tags on has the same function as so many of Wumen's comments, to signal to the reader that this is an exercise. The point is not to understand conceptually how or why past, present, and future mind cannot be grasped: The message is to use this line of scripture as a lens to focus attention in a novel way, in an attempt to reflect the ineffable in the mirror of consciousness.

One mistake intellectuals commonly make is not really trying to focus the mind in this way because they already know it is theoretically impossible to grasp the essence of mind anyway. The secret here is that the "cannot be grasped" refers to method, in the sense that it means not grasping thoughts as they come and go, and it also refers to state of awareness, in the sense that it means direct consciousness of the ethereal nature of awareness itself underlying all mental events.

In Zen lore, Zen adepts, especially concealed ones, commonly chide scholars and priests for not practicing what they study and preach. This is a classic example. Wumen says, "Faced with this question, Deshan could only frown." The conventional mind cannot even perceive, let alone handle, the vastness beyond its preconceived boundaries. "But even so," Wumen goes on, "he did not die at the woman's words," in the dual sense that he did not use this impasse to transcend his circle of assumptions and doubts all at once, nor did he let it destroy his last chance by allowing it to inflame his egotistic wrath. What he did do was continue his search for a Zen master, only now not to contend but to learn.

Deshan's "complete defeat," in Wumen's classical terms,

was the final submission of his limited intellect to the realization that infinity is not an idea but an experience. "His earlier words did not match his later talk" in the sense that the idea and the experience are not the same thing; as Wumen says in his verse, "Hearing the name is not like seeing the face, / Seeing the face is not like hearing the name."

Wumen concludes his prose comment with one of his usual warnings to get the essential point in the effect of the action, while avoiding entanglement in the superficial appearance of the story. When a Zen master is said to be "unconscious of being unseemly because of compassion for a child," it means that the method or technique of teaching employed is not a personal predilection but a temporary expedient devised for the needs of a particular individual or type of seeker.

To say that the Zen master is "unconscious of being unseemly" has several levels of meaning. In one sense, it means that imitations of his act ("unseemliness") are not part of his intention. In another sense it means that Zen masters are willing, when necessary, to employ means of teaching that cannot be understood in conventional terms (and are therefore "unseemly"). And it also means that the sayings and actions of Zen masters have covert ("unconscious") meanings that are often not at all what the sayings and actions seem to mean (so the surface event is "unseemly" in comparison to the inner intent).

At the conclusion of his verse comment, Wumen turns to an even higher level of integration of insight. Here he points out that cosmic consciousness is still only part of complete Zen enlightenment, and thus stories like this should not be taken to represent the whole issue: "Even though he managed to save his nostrils, / Nonetheless he blinded his eyes." As another Zen proverb says, "The heart of nirvana is relatively easy to attain; knowledge of differentiation is hard to clarify." The last lines of the verses of Zen master Baoning and Zen master Dahong also conclude with a reminder to the seeker to "see both sides" and fully integrate the heart of nirvana with objective knowledge of the world.

Not the Wind, Not the Banner

Once when the wind was whipping the banner of a temple, the Sixth Patriarch of Zen witnessed two monks debating about it. One said the banner was moving, one said the wind was moving.

They argued back and forth without attaining the principle, so the Patriarch said, "This is not the movement of the wind, nor the movement of the banner; it is the movement of your minds."

The two monks were both awestruck.

WUMEN SAYS,

It is not the wind moving, not the banner moving, not the mind moving: Where do you see the Zen patriarch? If you can see intimately here, then you will realize that the monks were buying iron but got gold, while the Zen patriarch, unable to conceal his enlightenment, divulged it on this occasion.

WUMEN'S VERSE

Wind, banner, minds moving—
Their crimes are listed on one indictment.
If you only know how to open your mouth,
You won't realize when you're trapped in words.

ZEN MASTER BALING SAID,

The Zen master said it is not the wind moving, and not the banner moving. If it is not the wind or the banner, where is it evident?

If there is anyone who can play the host for the Zen master, come forth and meet with me.

TRANSLATOR'S COMMENTS

The great Sixth Patriarch of Zen has already been seen in koan number twenty-three, "Not Thinking of Good or Evil." According to Zen lore, after he disappeared from sight to avoid the wrath of jealous clerics, the Sixth Patriarch lived among mountain hunters for fifteen years. The present koan is the traditional story of the occasion of his emerging from concealment.

The essential point of the story is to illustrate how we think about our thoughts and imagine we have thereby explained things. Judging by our conceptual constructions rather than by direct perceptions, we wind up entrapped in our own points of view. We may think we are talking about realities when all we are doing is talking about what we think. As the koan says, this can be a shocking realization.

In his prose comment, Wumen adds that it is not the mind moving either. Here he is not contradicting the Zen patriarch; he is making a pragmatic distinction between the essence of mind (which does not fluctuate) and the functions of mind (which do fluctuate). When Wumen asks, "Where do you see the Zen patriarch?" he refers to the essence of mind as it is in itself, not as it is refracted in fragmentary mental functions. This is what Zen master Baling means by calling for "anyone who can play the host for the Zen master," referring to the universal mind that is at the very root of all consciousness.

Wumen goes on to say that if you realize this universal mind, you see how the monks were buying iron but got gold: First, they were haggling over mental constructions but instead received witness of mind itself; and second, they were expecting to find an answer in the form of a metaphysical principle, but instead got their reply in the form of a direct insight.

Wumen's verse begins by describing the relativity of the perceived world and the perceiving mind. It ends by reminding us that if we only use our conceptualizing minds we will only get theoretical answers; if we want actual experience of understanding, we need understanding through actual experience. Zen master Baling's verse echoes the call to that in us which understands through direct experience. It is through inwardly asking ourselves the question he poses that the living meaning of Zen becomes the normal condition of consciousness.

30

The Very Mind Itself Is Buddha

Damei asked Mazu, "What is Buddha?"
Mazu said, "The very mind itself is Buddha."

WUMEN SAYS,
If you can get the point directly, you wear Buddha's clothing, eat Buddha's food, speak Buddha's language, do what Buddha does; that is, you are Buddha.

But even so, how many people has Damei drawn into mistakenly approving the zero point of the scale! How could they know to wash their mouths out for three days when they say the word "Buddha"? Had he been enlightened, he would have covered his ears and run away on being told that mind itself is Buddha.

WUMEN'S VERSE
On a clear day, in the bright sunlight,
Don't go searching around;
To go on asking "what"
Is to protest your innocence while holding the loot.

TRANSLATOR'S COMMENTS

Damei (pronounced Dah-may) and Mazu (pronounced Mah-dzoo) lived in the eighth century. Mazu was one of the greatest Zen masters of all time. He is said to have guided as many as one hundred and thirty-nine disciples to enlightenment.

There is little to be said about this koan. Wumen begins his prose comment as usual with a technical description of the experience of the koan. The apparently paradoxical statements in the second part of his comment warn against a typical misunderstanding, which is to construe "the very mind itself" to refer to the ordinary subjective mentality with its conditioned thought habits.

This traditional warning is issued with supreme clarity by the great Japanese Zen master Dogen in his commentary on this koan: "When they hear tell of 'mind itself,' what the ignorant suppose it means is that ordinary people's thinking awareness without awakened aspiration for enlightenment is itself Buddha. This is a consequence of never having met an enlightened teacher."

Thus the practice and understanding of Zen makes a distinction between the false mind and the true mind; this is utterly critical for Zen realization. The main difficulty in Zen, from this point of view, is to give up seeking for a theoretically imagined enlightenment in order to experience the mind in its natural purity by direct intuitive insight and spontaneous understanding.

31

Zhaozhou Checks a Woman

A monk asked a woman, "Which way is the road to the sacred mountain Taishan?"

The woman said, "Go right straight ahead."

When the monk had gone a few steps, the woman said, "A fine monk—and so he goes!"

Later a monk told Zhaozhou about this. Zhaozhou said, "Wait till I check out this woman for you."

The next day Zhaozhou went and asked her the same question; and the woman also answered in the same way. Zhaozhou returned and said to his group, "I have checked out the woman of Taishan for you."

WUMEN SAYS,

The woman only knew how to sit there and scheme in her tent, unaware when she ran into a rebel. As for old Zhaozhou, he skillfully used the device of sneaking into the camp and removing the barricades; but he had none of the marks of great people. When you bring them up for examination, both of them had faults.

But tell me, at what point did Zhaozhou check out the woman?

WUMEN'S VERSE

Since the question was the same,
The reply was also similar.
There is sand in the rice,
Thorns in the mud.

ZEN MASTER FENYANG'S VERSE

Old Lady Zen on the road to the holy Mount Tai—
South, North, East, West—myriad myriad thousand.
Zhaozhou's checking people is hard to understand—
Coming and going, his straw sandals were worn clear
   through.

ZEN MASTER HUANGLONG NAN'S VERSE

Outstanding from the community is Zhaozhou;
The woman's test was out of the blue.
Now the four seas are clear as mirrors;
Let travelers not make enemies of the road.

ZEN MASTER YUNXI'S VERSE

On the road to Taishan, a white-headed woman;
Endless travelers have passed by, how many times!
Of the hidden gate to the direct way, people are not aware;
So Zhaozhou made a special trip to cut off the confusion.

ZEN MASTER TUSHUAI'S VERSE

Go right straight ahead, go right straight ahead,
Not following the pointing finger itself, not going the same
   old way:
People who are robust and hardy
Walk alone in the universe.

TRANSLATOR'S COMMENTS

Taishan is Mount Wutai, the northern of the Five Holy Mountains of China. It was believed to be an abode of the great Buddhist saint Manjushri (pronounced Mon-joo-shree), who is the supernal personification of wisdom in Buddhist iconography. At the time of this story, Taishan drew countless pilgrims, even from as far away as India.

This koan is about "testing" and "checking," like the early one about the same master Zhaozhou testing two hermits; so it can really fool you if you do not have independent vision.

This koan is also about the integration of practice and realization, so it can show whether you are in the habit of forcing conclusions where there are only processes.

In very simple terms, a central issue revolves around the way one interprets "right straight ahead"—literally or figuratively. The Zen master Zhaozhou certainly demonstrates a straightforward approach to the question raised.

Wumen begins his prose comment in one of his usual ways, with a crack that looks like criticism but basically describes an essential point or state of the koan in a functional or technical manner. What he means is that the type of device the woman used can only expose those who respond to it, and does not necessarily reveal anything about those who do not.

Wumen goes on to treat the Zen master in the same way, acknowledging his mastery of probing technique, especially noting Zhaozhou's unobtrusive subtlety ("he had none of the marks of great people"), which could be extremely effective under the right circumstances, but could also go completely unnoticed and therefore be in that sense useless for study.

Wumen concludes this portion of his prose comment with the remark that there exist incompleteness and ambiguity in both the method of the woman and the method of Zhaozhou, for the reasons just described. Of course, that very realization is itself incomplete and ambiguous, which is why it puts us to the test. Thus Wumen goes ahead and asks the reader, "At what point did Zhaozhou check out the woman?"

Wumen's verse comment begins with a lulling truism, mirroring the apparent everyday ordinariness of the action in the koan. Then he suddenly states the shocking reality that it is not as simple as it seems, that there are unexpected complications in the Zen master's test.

Although it is traditionally considered very difficult, there is something about this koan that is obvious for those who have already seen koan number eleven about testing hermits. But there is also an extra subtlety in this koan, although it is one that is also obvious when you see it. It is better for the reader to see this independently, but I have quoted the verses of four Zen masters to help.

For the purposes of illustration, I combine the final lines of these four verses into a single poem, to show something about the living meaning of this koan:

Zhaozhou made a special trip to cut off the confusion;
Coming and going, his sandals were worn clear through.
Let travelers not make enemies of the road;
Walk alone in the universe.

An Outsider Questions Buddha

An outsider questioned Buddha in these terms: "I do not ask about the spoken, I do not ask about the unspoken."

The Buddha just sat there.

The outsider said in praise, "World Honored One, you are very kind, very compassionate; opening up the clouds of my confusion, you have enabled me to attain penetration." Then he paid respects and left.

Ananda subsequently asked Buddha, "What did the outsider realize, that he uttered this praise and left?"

Buddha said, "Like a good horse, he goes as soon as he sees the mere shadow of the whip."

WUMEN SAYS,
Ananda was a disciple of Buddha, but even so he did not match the outsider's insight.

Now tell me, how far apart are an outsider and a disciple of Buddha?

WUMEN'S VERSE

Walking on a sword blade,
Running on an ice edge,
Without going through any steps
He lets go over a cliff.

ZEN MASTER BAIYUN'S VERSE

Ten thousand fathoms deep, the cold pool is clear to the
  very bottom;
A brocade carp in the still of the night travels toward the
  light.
With a tug of the pole, it comes up, following the hook;
On the surface of the water, indistinct, the light of the
  moon is scattered.

ZEN MASTER BAONING'S VERSE

Night fell on him passing by, so he lodged in the wild
  weeds;
When he managed to open his eyes, the sky was completely
  light.
With an empty heart and bare feet, he goes back home
  singing;
On the road the travelers already are not few.

ZEN MASTER GUMU'S VERSE

Snow covering a deciduous forest, all is one color;
Clear light above and below engulfs the sky.
A wood gatherer stands at the ford, cold;
For whom is the distant full moon white?

TRANSLATOR'S COMMENTS

In Buddhist literature, an "outsider" overtly refers to a non-Buddhist, especially a non-Buddhist philosopher or religious mendicant. In Zen symbolic language, "outsiders" are those who are unaware of the Buddha-nature within their essential minds and therefore cling to something "outside." In this case, everything is "outside," even abstract ideas about the nature of ultimate truth.

The question posed by the outsider in this koan refers to what Buddhists call emptiness, a reference to ultimate truth. The great illuminate Nagarjuna defined emptiness as "departure from all views." The outsider's indirect reference to the "spoken" and the "unspoken" is a traditional way of referring to the totality of all possible notions about reality, all that can be conceived as well as all that is beyond conception. In simpler terms, the outsider asks the Buddha if there is any realization that transcends understanding of the relative world and the absolute truth.

The classical Buddhist definition of emptiness as "departure from all views" means, for one thing, that fixed ideas and opinions crowd consciousness and blind the clarity of direct insight. Buddhism often illustrates the limitations of all categories of thought, in order to shift attention to a more direct yet more comprehensive mode of awareness. This is what the "outsider" was getting at: how to make the leap from the boundaries of conceptual consciousness into the infinity of enlightened knowledge.

In reply, "The Buddha just sat there." A number of koans are built on this very same model; and the traditional warning of the masters is this: "Don't go to the silence to understand." In the great Nagarjuna's classical statement just cited, after defining "emptiness" as "departure from all views," he immediately adds, "but those who hold to the view of emptiness cannot be saved." This is an incalculably important point, as the rest of the koan demonstrates.

The outsider in the story obviously did not take Buddha's silence as silence (for that would have been about the spoken or unspoken); as Buddha himself said, "He goes as soon as he sees the mere shadow of the whip." Buddha's silence, in other words, is an indirect teaching, a "shadow of the whip," not negation or assent, but a "penetration" of all subjective ideas of any kind. Look *through* the window, not *at* it.

As Wumen notes in his prose comment, Ananda was a disciple of Buddha. In history, Ananda was Buddha's secretary and memorized many of Buddha's discourses; so in Zen iconography, Ananda represents formal learning. The point of Wumen's comparison between Ananda and the outsider is that formal learning does not in itself realize the same effect as direct insight.

Summing up as usual with a question to bring the koan alive, Wumen asks how far apart an outsider and a disciple of Buddha are. On the one hand, he asks us to see how a "disciple of Buddha" can be an outsider by attachment to dogmatic understanding. On the other hand, he asks us to see how an "outsider" can become a disciple of Buddha by direct awakening to the naturally real.

Wumen's verse comment is exceptionally sharp, illustrating the keen focus of the exercise represented by the outsider's question, and the swift response of the effect represented by the outsider's reaction to Buddha's reply.

As for the beautiful verse comments of other Zen masters on this prototypical koan, in spite of their colorful surface content, they can be understood quite readily as structural analyses of the koan.

The first two lines of Zen master Baiyun's verse describe the state of the outsider as he came to Buddha. The third line refers to the Buddha simultaneously testing and teaching the outsider. The last line acknowledges the awakening of the outsider, but makes careful note of the fact that no "content" of the awakening is specifically expressed, and warns the reader not to project any subjective ideas on the outsider's insight.

The first line of Zen master Baoning's verse symbolizes the technical definition of an "outsider" as someone in the "night" ("dark") of ignorance, lost in the "wild weeds" of arbitrary thoughts and subjective ideas. The second line describes his awakening as the realization that ultimate reality is of itself clear ("the sky was completely light"), having been obscured only by our subjective imaginings. The third line depicts the outsider after his awakening, now liberated from the burden of subjective views. The last line affirms that this potential is in everyone, and also leaves a typically subtle reminder to avoid thinking of the Buddha's reply and the outsider's realization as a state of empty nothingness.

Zen master Gumu's verse begins with symbolic reference to vision of total unity of being (line one) and insight into absolute emptiness (line two). Then he goes on to describe the outsider having left aside all of his intellectual holdings (line three), and concludes with an invitation to the reader to look into the root of the matter, the essence of mind.

33

Not Mind, Not Buddha

A monk asked Mazu, "What is Buddha?"
Mazu said, "Not mind, not Buddha."

WUMEN SAYS,
If you can see this, you are a graduate of Zen.

WUMEN'S VERSE
When you meet a swordsman on the road, draw;
If you do not meet a poet, don't recite.
When you meet people, tell thirty percent;
Don't give away the whole thing.

ZEN MASTER DAHUI'S VERSE
"Mind itself is Buddha"—don't seek arbitrarily.
"Not mind, not Buddha"—stop searching elsewhere.
Snowflakes fly over the flames of a glowing furnace:
A dot of coolness removes the torment of the heat.

TRANSLATOR'S COMMENTS

The great master Mazu was met in koan number thirty, "The Very Mind Itself Is Buddha."

In the simplest possible terms, "Not mind, not Buddha" means Buddhahood is not the temporally conditioned mentality with its compulsive habits of thought, and is not any idea or image of "Buddha" that this mentality can conceive.

In an even deeper pragmatic sense, "not mind" refers to detachment from thoughts, "not Buddha" refers to detachment from undifferentiated clarity as a mental state or object in itself.

The next step cannot be communicated directly from one person to another, because it is the individual's first-hand experience of real suchness.

In another koan connected with this famous line of teaching, Mazu explains how the teaching that "mind is Buddha" represents an expedient technique to stop confused imagination and wishful thinking about Buddhahood: A seeker asked Mazu, "Why do you say mind is Buddha?"

Mazu said, "To get children to stop crying."

The seeker asked, "After the crying stops, then what?"

Mazu said, "Not mind, not Buddha."

Wumen's one-line prose comment seems completely straightforward, but like most such Zen sayings it contains a concealed "hook." According to many Zen classics, at every stage of the Way some people come to feel that what they have experienced is all there is. Does a graduate of Zen still have anything to learn?

Wumen's verse comment describes the advanced study of the infinite knowledge of differentiation in suchness. This includes the science of objective communication, which requires a Zen master to discern the level of an individual's understanding in order to establish meaningful interaction leading to a meeting of minds.

This comment also hints that we should avoid trying to apply koans like this out of order, which is exactly what happens when sayings like "mind is Buddha" turn into dogma and cliché.

Wumen concludes with another multiple *entendre* alluding to the endless infinity of reality, the impossibility of capturing everything in words, and the need for people to experience direct perception of reality themselves in order to attain full understanding of what little can be hinted about it.

The verse of Zen master Dahui summarizes these points. In the first line he says that "Mind itself is Buddha" was a teaching designed to still the restless mind seeking an imagined reality. But there were yet those who went on to try to understand this Buddha-mind by thinking about it with their own thoughts, so "Not mind, not Buddha" was then presented to halt even abstract seeking.

Dahui's verse ends with a description of the feeling and effect engendered in consciousness when deliberately focusing attention on this koan to alert the mind: "Snowflakes" (random thoughts) may "fly," but if they fly over the "flames of a glowing furnace" (absorption in focus on "not mind, not Buddha"), then the flying "snowflake" thoughts spontaneously vaporize in the "flames of concentration." Reversing the image but producing the same meaning (a Zen device to prevent drowsiness), Dahui describes this koan meditation as like a "dot of coolness" that "removes the torment of the heat" of confused thoughts.

34

Knowledge Is Not the Way

Nanquan said, "Mind is not Buddha, knowledge is not the Way."

WUMEN SAYS,
It might be said of Nanquan that he was so old he had no shame; the minute he opened his foul mouth he advertised the family disgrace. Even so, few are those who know enough to be grateful.

WUMEN'S VERSE
When the sky clears, the sun emerges;
When it rains, the ground gets wet.
He wholeheartedly told it all,
Only fearing incomplete faith.

TRANSLATOR'S COMMENTS

Nanquan has already been met, in koan fourteen, "Killing a Cat," and koan nineteen, "The Normal Is the Way." Appropriately, Nanquan was a disciple of Mazu, and this koan follows up on the point of the preceding one.

As he so often does, Wumen starts out with a deliberately misleading tone of sarcasm. What he is really saying underneath is that all reference to the absolute is by nature relative. Zen teaching masters can only hint at reality and demonstrate means of perceiving it, but the actual experience of insight is up to the individual.

Wumen again concludes with a challenge, declaring that few people realize that Nanquan's statement of the limitations of human understanding is actually intended to clear the way for insight into a much more subtle experience of reality. Wumen's verse invites us into the experience left unspoken by the ancient master, and reiterates his concern that we take it up for ourselves.

For this koan we are blessed with the rare fortune of having the explanation of Zen master Nanquan himself, which I translate directly from the ancient record of his teaching:

The Way is the Great Way without obstacles; subtle action free from passion is inherently complete. Only thus do you attain freedom in all domains of activity. Therefore we speak of acting without attachment to objects in all domains of activity, and we also refer to absorption in unlimited action, manifesting physical forms everywhere.

Just because it is unknown to others, this function has

no tracks and does not belong to the realms of perception or cognition. Truth is realized spontaneously, subtle functions are fulfilled spontaneously. The Great Way is formless, truth is beyond comparison. Therefore they do not belong to perception or cognition.

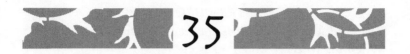

A Woman's Split Soul

Wuzu asked a monk, "A woman split her soul; which was the real one?"

WUMEN SAYS,
If you can understand the real one here, you will know that leaving a shell and entering a shell is like lodging at an inn.

If not, it is essential that you do not run off at random. When the material body disintegrates all at once, you will be like a lobster in hot water, frantically thrashing about. At that time, don't say I didn't tell you.

WUMEN'S VERSE
The clouds and moon are the same,
The valleys and mountains are individually different.
Myriad blessings, myriad blessings—
Are they one or two?

ZEN MASTER PURONG'S VERSE

The dual woman combines the roles of daughter and wife:
When the wheel of potential is cut off, interchange is
  impossible.
All along the comings and goings have no tracks;
Travelers are not to be asked the road by which they came.

ZEN MASTER CISHOU'S VERSE

It is just the usual carryings-on;
Casually brought up, it becomes confusing.
Last night a wild wind arose,
Blowing down who knows how many peach blossoms.

ZEN MASTER HUO-AN'S VERSE

Whatever is done is not forgotten
Even in thousands of years:
When causes and conditions combine,
Results and consequences are naturally experienced.

TRANSLATOR'S COMMENTS

Zen master Wuzu died in 1104. He came to Zen practice when he was already a middle-aged man, and his general iconographical significance in Zen lore is seen in his robust earthiness and practicality, transformed into spiritual tools through Zen enlightenment. Noted for his inimitable style, Wuzu used all sorts of interesting and arresting devices to teach people. He is, for this reason, one of those Zen masters whose teachings are considered paragons of misdirection and inscrutability, traditional arts of warfare and political strategy which are transmuted by Zen spiritual "alchemy" into tactics of Zen teaching, whose object is to communicate the ineffable.

In the koan at hand, the "woman who split her soul" is the heroine of a folk story well known to the Chinese people of Wuzu's time. The underlying point of the tale is that human beings play different roles in life, and relate differently to different people and different situations through these different roles. Wuzu's question is this: "Who and what is the real self underlying and undertaking these roles?"

The Zen point is that these roles are not the real self, but are more properly like guests or servants of the real self. Confusion and loss of freedom arise from a fundamental misapprehension: Identifying with a role, people can forget and lose the rest of their potential; shifting from role to role unconscious of the central "pivot" of the essential self, people can experience stultifying conflicts among their commitments to different roles.

Zen teaches a personality-transcending experiential standpoint from which it is possible to attain independent insight and restore elements of personality to their proper function as servants rather than masters of mind. Wumen's prose comment deals with realizing the essential nature of mind; his verse comment places this in the context of life in the world, while maintaining the critical discernment of the distinction between the essential and circumstantial.

The first two of the other Zen comments begin from the perspective of the relative, the stream of events and nexus of conditions that gives the appearance of so many faces of existence. Then they turn to the absolute to realize freedom of spirit untrammeled by changes in temporal states of being.

Zen master Purong (pronounced Poo-zroong) uses the image of the two roles in the story, which naturally are two universal roles in spite of the fact that they are actualized in many different ways. He goes on to warn us not to lose touch with the source, lest we lose communion and harmony among the different selves we act out. In the third line, Purong turns to the experience of the essence of mind, in which the "comings and goings" of fluctuations in emotions and thoughts "have no tracks" and do not leave a binding influence. The final line is a beautiful expression of the transcendence of essential mind, the eternal Buddhanature, over all the temporal roles that humans can play out.

The verse of Zen master Cishou (pronounced Tsih-sho) affirms that ordinary social life normally involves the performance of different roles, putting on and taking off different masks. When we do not understand the real nature of what we are doing, he continues, we become confused by our own act. In the third line Cishou presents a colorful description of Wuzu's questioning the ultimate reality of social roles, acting like a "wild wind" that "blows down" the "peach blossoms" of conceited fancies about these roles.

The last verse, by Zen master Huo-an shows how "personalities," including all facets of life, evolve through action. This has a dual meaning, in reference to bondage and to liberation. On the one hand, it means that whatever you do there is no escaping the consequences of that action, because it affects the development of *all* of your personalities in some way, and also affects other people. On the other hand, it means that when you attain the transcendental viewpoint of Zen, you do not efface everything and abandon the world; liberation means that you can now act independently and constructively, uninhibited by identification with a fixed set of feelings and thoughts.

This is what Mahayana Buddhism calls the creation of "mentally produced bodies," the development of expanded and diversified personalities and capabilities for the purpose of carrying out beneficial and enlightening tasks in the world.

36

Meeting Adepts on the Road

Wuzu said, "On the road, when you encounter people who have attained the Way, you do not face them with speech or silence. So tell me, how do you face them?"

WUMEN SAYS,
If you can answer intimately here, that will no doubt be a joy and a pleasure; but if not, you should keep an eye out everywhere.

WUMEN'S VERSE
On the road, meeting people who've attained the Way,
You do not face them with speech or silence:
Punch them right in the jaw;
If they understand directly, then they understand.

ZEN MASTER YUELIN'S VERSE
Those who come talking about right and wrong
Are themselves right and wrong people:
How true are these words!
Sport with things unconcerned with their names.

TRANSLATOR'S COMMENTS

This is the same master Wuzu as in the preceding koan, again presenting a problem to force the mind into a higher level of psychological integration than is possible by self-limiting discriminatory "either/or" thinking. In the preceding koan, the master asked us to see a level of mind deeper than "either/or" choices. In this koan he asks us to see the ineffable beyond "neither/nor."

The easiest way to see this koan is to use Wumen's admonition to "keep an eye out everywhere." Try to notice everything all around you as a total field of awareness for a period of ten days or so; then you may well see for yourself why what you experience cannot be expressed in words, yet cannot be relegated to silence.

Wumen's "punch in the jaw" is not intended literally. It is an expression of the dynamic experience of direct encounter with the real. When he says, "If they understand directly, then they understand," Wumen reaffirms the technical caveat that this experience is only realized by direct insight, not conceptual thinking.

The verse of Zen master Yuelin declares the apparent conundrum to be itself a construction of the subjective mind, a reflection of the human mentality rather than a property of objective reality. He concludes with a very practical and down-to-earth method of integrating realization of absolute and relative truths in the living reality of everyday life: "Sport with things unconcerned with their names."

37

The Cypress Tree in the Yard

A monk asked Zhaozhou, "What is the living meaning of Zen?"

Zhaozhou said, "The cypress tree in the yard."

WUMEN SAYS,
If you can see the point of Zhaozhou's answer intimately, there is no past Buddha before and no future Buddha after.

WUMEN'S VERSE
Words do not set forth facts,
Speech does not accord with situations;
Those who take up words perish,
Those who linger over sayings get lost.

ZEN MASTER HUANGLONG NAN'S VERSE
All trees wither and die in time,
But the cypress in Zhaozhou's yard flourishes forever.
Not only does it defy the frost, keeping its integrity;
It virtually sings with a clear voice to the light of the moon.

ZEN MASTER FOGUO BAI'S VERSE

Only when really unusual do you recognize the unusual;
It is the eye of spirits that recognizes spirits.
People today don't know the living meaning of Zen;
They only see the green green cypress in the yard.

ZEN MASTER FOJIAN'S VERSE

When the rain clears in the vast and endless sky,
The bright moon shines with a clear radiance.
Floating clouds cover up a thousand people's eyes;
Those who see the face on the moon are few and far
* between.*

TRANSLATOR'S COMMENTS

Zen master Zhaozhou is already a familiar figure. His saying in this koan is a reflection of the suchness of being-as-is. In his prose comment, Wumen says that if you see the point intimately, there is no past Buddha before and no future Buddha after: In other words, the immediate moment of awareness of suchness is the Buddha of all time.

In his verse comment, Wumen warns us not to mistake ordinary conditioned perceptions for true suchness itself. Undoubtedly the plainness and rigor of Wumen's statement here is adopted in view of the deceptively simple face of the koan, often noted by Zen commentators.

In contrast, the verse of Zen master Huanglong Nan is a beautiful eulogy of the eternal reality of suchness and its accessibility to clear awareness.

The verse of Zen master Foguo Bai (pronounced Faw-gwaw Bye) emphasizes the practical need for clarifying awareness, so that it is possible to actually see suchness as is. He says that most people who hear of the identity of samsara and nirvana mistake their ordinary experience for true suchness, and thus wind up every bit as attached to objects as any ordinary person.

Finally, the verse of Fojian begins with another description of the preliminary need for mental clarification before objective insight is possible. Then he turns to depict the condition of the ordinary human mentality as being clouded with subjective views and opinions, thus rarely seeing truth as it is.

38

The Ox Passing Through the Window Screen

Wuzu said, "It is as if an ox had passed through a window screen: Its head, horns, and four hooves have all passed through; why can't the tail pass through?"

WUMEN SAYS,
If here you can shift into reverse, set a single eye, and speak a pivotal word, you will be able to requite the favors you receive and help all beings. Otherwise, you have to pay further attention to the tail before you get it.

WUMEN'S VERSE
If it goes on past, it falls into a pit;
If it comes back, then it is spoiled.
This little tail
Is very strange indeed.

TRANSLATOR'S COMMENTS

Here is another one of Wuzu's devilish schemes. Japanese Zen masters consider this koan one of the most difficult to penetrate, so they usually take it up in a comparatively advanced stage of study. One reason for this is that the question involves examination of very subtle barriers to enlightenment. In advanced Zen, special attention is focused on the problem of mental obstruction by the feeling of knowing, or being conscious of consciousness.

In my opinion, perhaps the best illustration of this sense of the koan may be made by parallel. As it happens, there is an excellent parallel in the story of Wuzu's own completion of the awakening process.

Wuzu had already studied with ten Zen masters before he came to Master Baiyun, and he was under the impression that he had understood and realized Zen. His object in continuing Zen studies was to test himself and also to test the masters.

One day Baiyun told him that several Zen practitioners had just arrived, adding that all of them had experienced Zen awakening, could explain it, could understand Zen stories, and could comment on them. Pausing a while, Master Baiyun finally said, "But they're still inadequate. You tell me why."

Many readers will by now recognize the working of the Zen "hook" to bring hidden doubts and confusion to the surface. This is not an arbitrary challenge, however, since the experiences and capacities Baiyun describes are really not the totality of Buddhist enlightenment. What he wanted was for Wuzu to question this, in principle and in himself.

As it turned out, Wuzu was in fact deeply disturbed by

the statement of Zen master Baiyun. Unable to fathom this mystery, he wondered about it constantly for seven days. Finally one night he understood, the story goes, and all at once "let go of what he had been treasuring," forgetting his subjective feeling of completeness and realizing the true infinity of enlightenment.

This is what is called "the wind of unburdening" in Zen language. It is what you turn to when you realize why "the tail hasn't passed through."

For the beginner, there is an easier way to approach this koan. Something of the point can be seen by the following procedure:

a) Forget thoughts, even as they occur.
b) Use the leeway thus created to let the mind merge with space as a total field of awareness.
c) View the totality itself as the "tail" that has "not yet passed through."
d) Observe the consciousness of awareness itself as the "tail that has not yet passed through."

In Wumen's comments, which are appropriately abstruse for this koan, to "shift into reverse" means to detach from absorption in nirvana, "set a single eye" to see the transcendental peace of nirvana right in the midst of samsara, and be able to express this transformation of ordinary experience into enlightened awareness. If you cannot do this, he concludes, you should turn your attention back to the "tail," which here means your own mind.

In his verse comment, Wumen expresses a dual meaning. One meaning is in reference to nirvana, the other in reference to suchness. Referring to nirvana, he says that if we go too far, if we understand transcendence as complete separation, then we "fall into a pit." But if we come back from transcendent experience only to resume former habits of thought, then the value of nirvana is "spoiled."

Referring to suchness, Wumen says that if we go too far, if we identify ordinary perceptions with suchness, then we fall into a pit of ordinary biases and attachments. But if we resort to permanent nirvana as quiescence, the living potential of freedom is spoiled.

From either point of view, "This little tail / Is very strange indeed"! In one sense, "strange" means wonderful; with our minds we can become enlightened, or we can become deluded. In another sense, "strange" means unlike anything else; the essence of mind in itself is not identical, and not even like in kind, to any thing that may be imagined. It is essential to be aware of this kind of "strangeness" in Zen work.

39

Trapped in Words

A monk asked Yunmen about the line, "Radiant light silently illumines the universe."

Before the monk had even finished, Yunmen abruptly said, "Aren't these the words of the scholar Zhang Zhuo?"

The monk replied, "Yes."

Yunmen said, "You're trapped in words."

Later, Zen master Sixin brought this up and said, "Now tell me, where did the monk get trapped in words?"

WUMEN SAYS,

If you can see the radical strictness of Yunmen's action, and why the monk got bogged down in words, then you can be a teacher of humans and celestial spirits. But if you still do not understand, you cannot even save yourself.

WUMEN'S VERSE

He casts his hook in the swift current;
One greedy for the bait bites.
As soon as the seam of his mouth opens,
He's lost his natural life.

ZEN MASTER SUSHAN'S VERSE

Questioning, answering, free from partiality:
How can an iron wall or silver mountain be penetrated?
Conceding and denying depend on the time; he says "You're
  trapped in words,"
Eventually causing a thousand ages to stir the wind of
  lament.

ZEN MASTER SONGYUAN'S VERSE

Clearly he depicts it for you to see:
The meaning is on the hook, not in the pan.
Even if a stone man can open his mouth,
He still doesn't realize he's been fooled by his tongue.

TRANSLATOR'S COMMENTS

Zen master Yunmen has already been seen in several koans. Zhang Zhuo (pronounced Jong-jwaw) was a noted poet who was also interested in Zen. Sixin (pronounced Sih-shin) was a distinguished master of the Linji school of Zen who lived about a century before Wumen.

To understand Yunmen's testing device, it is crucial to note the question posed by Sixin. If you can see the answer to this question, at what point the monk got trapped in words, you can learn to use words without getting trapped.

In order to see the answer to this question, particularly note Songyuan's comment, "The meaning is on the hook, not in the pan." Was the monk already trapped in words, only to be exposed by the master? Or was the monk trapped in words by the master's question? Either way, he found out how easily it can happen, "causing a thousand ages to stir the wind of lament."

Wumen's comments describe the comprehensive perspective of Yunmen and the nature of his action as a test. The verse of Zen master Sushan depicts the surface impenetrability of the simple factuality of the initial exchange between Yunmen and the monk. Because similar appearances may disguise different realities, it takes the device of a Zen master to see if a questioner is true or false.

The verse of Zen master Songyuan is unusually explicit, miming the deceptive simplicity of the koan. He lauds the clarity with which Yunmen's device exposes the monk. Songyuan also reveals the secret of Zen testing methods, which is based on the nature of the relationship between subject and object.

Songyuan's final lines represent the monk's getting caught without even realizing it. This is a typical warning to the reader to pay special attention to see just where the trap is. Where is it now?

40

Kicking Over a Water Pitcher

Master Guishan started out in the community of Master Baizhang serving as the chief cook. Baizhang was going to appoint him to be the master of Great Gui Mountain, and so requested him and the leader of the assembly to utter a saying to the community, in order that the most extraordinary individual could be the one to go.

Baizhang picked up a water pitcher, set it on a rock, and posed this question: "If you cannot call it a water pitcher, what do you call it?"

The leader of the assembly said, "It cannot be called a wooden upright bolt."

Baizhang then asked Guishan. Guishan immediately kicked over the pitcher and left.

Baizhang smiled and said, "The leader of the assembly has lost the mountain." And so he had Guishan start Zen teaching on that mountain.

WUMEN SAYS,
Guishan was courageous, but he could not leap clear of Baizhang's snare. When you bring the matter up for examination, he finds convenience in the heavy, not in

the light. How so? Look! He removed his bandanna and took up iron fetters.

WUMEN'S VERSE
Tossing aside his basket and ladle,
He gives a direct thrust, no beating around the bush.
Baizhang's double barrier cannot stop him;
The point of his foot kicks out Buddhas without number.

ZEN MASTER SHAOZHAO'S VERSE
What determines the hero is the water jug;
At the point of minutest distinction, there are no more
  emotions.
Great peace is originally for the general to bring about,
But the general is not allowed to see great peace.

ZEN MASTER TONGZHAO'S VERSE
The great function needs an expert to know;
On the spot, one kick put an end to doubt.
What a pity those who do not succeed in Zen
Do nothing but judge right and wrong at the jug.

TRANSLATOR'S COMMENTS

Zen master Baizhang was met with in the second koan on "not being blind to cause and effect." Guishan was among the very greatest of Baizhang's many Zen successors. He was the author of one of the earliest written works on Zen, in which he teaches both sudden and gradual methods of enlightenment. Many koans about Guishan are found in classical collections.

The koan at hand is represented as the story of Guishan's final "graduation" from Baizhang's school. Ancient Chinese Zen schools did not cling to particular places, but spread all over the land, appearing when circumstances were appropriate and disappearing when their work was over.

The essential point of the koan as it is presented here is quite clear: In the life of Zen enlightenment, pragmatic measures prevail over theoretical disquisitions. Because this emphasis may mislead the superficial into fixation on dramatic acts, however, Wumen makes a joke of the koan's conclusion. In a humorous twist, he points out that Guishan was assigned a much more difficult and demanding responsibility because he got caught showing his enlightenment

The verse of Zen master Shaozhao (pronounced Shao-djao) begins by saying that the "water jug" stands for objective reality, indirectly affirming that Baizhang's decision to appoint Guishan as the new teacher was not based on subjective feelings or opinions. Shaozhao then cites the proverb, "Great peace is originally for the general to bring about, but the general is not allowed to see great peace." This means that Zen enlightenment is attained through one's own efforts, but not for the sake of individual ease. According to the universal vow of Buddhism, the enlightened do not spend the rest of their lives enjoying their own liberty, but dedicate it to the enlightenment of others.

The first line of the verse of Zen master Tongzhao (pronounced Toong-djao) refers to Guishan, and also to Baizhang. The "great function" means the activation of ordinarily unused potential in order to accomplish extraordinary acts of exertion and perception. In reference to Guishan, it means that one needs this great function as a prerequisite for taking up the responsibility of Zen teacherhood, which is to liberate minds from binding limitations ingrained by routine conventions of thought. In reference to Baizhang, it means that genuine direct perception is required in order to see whether someone else is acting on genuine direct perception.

The second line of the verse refers to Guishan's straightforward action that "put an end to doubt" by settling the ambiguities suggested in the first line.

The third line turns to the trap concealed in the action, which is then defined in the last line. The sense of these two lines is that those who are diverted or deceived by superficial appearances do not get the enlightenment of Zen from their interpretations of events. This distinguishes Zen from competitive educational systems that use promotion as an inducement to conformity.

Baizhang wanted a Zen center that pulsed from its own enlightened heart, not a mere clone or branch of his own school. This is why he did not appoint the senior disciple, but devised a special way of bringing out a truly exceptional successor.

41

Pacifying the Mind

As the founder of Zen faced a wall, his future successor stood in the snow, cut off his arm, and said, "My mind is not yet at peace. Please pacify my mind."

The founder said, "Bring me your mind, and I will pacify it for you."

The successor said, "I have looked for my mind, and cannot find it."

The founder said, "I have pacified your mind for you."

WUMEN SAID,

The founder of Zen sailed thousands of miles over the ocean, coming to China by stages; this might be called "raising waves without wind." In the end he got a student, but he turned out to be handicapped. Too bad! "The imbecile doesn't even know the motto on a penny."

WUMEN'S VERSE

Coming from the West, directly pointing,
The matter arose from entrusting a charge.
Stirring up the Zen communities,
After all it's you.

ZEN MASTER FENYANG'S VERSE

Nine years the founder faced a wall, awaiting the proper
* potential;*
Standing in snow up to his waist, the successor never
* relaxed his brow;*
Respectfully he asked for a method to pacify the mind:
Searching for the mind and not finding it, for the first time
* in his life he was free from doubt.*

ZEN MASTER FOGUO BAI'S VERSE

Thinking, why seek to pacify mind?
Seeking out peace of mind causes pain to the body.
Three feet deep the snow where he once stood:
Who knows who it is in the snow?

TRANSLATOR'S COMMENTS

The "founder of Zen" in this story was an Indian master named Bodhidharma, whose name means "The Way of Enlightenment" and is emblematic of the essential point of the founding of Zen as well as symbolic of the Zen mind itself.

At the time that the Zen founder was in China, which was between the late fifth century and the early sixth century, intellectual Buddhist studies were flourishing, but the Zen way of direct intuition was virtually unknown.

The story at hand, which is a popular elementary koan, symbolizes one of the basic exercises of Zen meditation, commonly called "turning the light around and looking backward." This is done by turning attention "backward" to the source of consciousness, rather than reaching "forward" to grasp at contents of consciousness.

In the koan, the successor awakens after realizing why he cannot find his mind. The pragmatic significance of this point is crucial, because only after having made this inward search for the source of consciousness is it possible to attain peace of mind by experiential realization of the ungraspability of mind. The end result of this exercise involves an experience of transformation from a sense of opacity and limitation to a sense of light and openness, with fresh awareness and understanding.

Wumen's prose comment conceals a technical analysis within a seemingly superficial critique. The expression "raising waves without wind," made in reference to the founding of Zen in China by a missionary from India, means that talk about "Zen" gives the impression that there is something special or exotic, something "extra" not shared by everyone, but in reality it deals with truths that are fundamental and apply in some basic sense to everyone everywhere regardless of culture or personality.

Wumen's remarks about the successor also seem to be derogatory quips, while concealing an essential provision about the exercise represented in this koan. The successor is called "handicapped" not because of the loss of his arm, but because this exercise deals exclusively with formless awareness, which is only one aspect of complete Zen enlightenment. It does not deal with knowledge of differentiation or understanding of objective causality, so the successor who symbolizes the exercise is called an "imbecile" who does not even know the simplest conventional facts.

Then again, the fact that the successor is called an imbecile unaware of conventional reality is also a signal that the exercise of looking into the mind is not a kind of self-analysis of the personality, but a direct activation of a deeper level of awareness.

The verse of Zen master Fenyang alludes to the story that the Zen founder sat silently facing a wall for nine years awaiting someone capable of understanding his teaching. When the successor finally came to him, the founder sat silently until the seeker had stood there through a snowstorm and cut off his arm. This symbolizes the learning of Zen in the process of going through the hardships of life in the world and cutting off illusions about the self in order to seek objective reality. The final line is a description of the method and realization of "turning the light around" and seeing the original mind.

The verse of Zen master Foguo Bai is extremely clever in conveying the orientation of the mind in the meditation represented by this concentration. In this sense "causing pain to the body" does not refer to the successor's austerities: It means directing the front-edge attention away from the material world.

"Three feet deep the snow where he once stood" means that the material world does not disappear after liberation; it is just that there are no more fixations on objects in the mind.

The final question employs the usual tactic of turning the work over to the reader, to see by direct perception: to see who it is in the snow, and also to see who knows who it is in the snow.

This last line is particularly clever in starting the reader off on the exercise in one of its most accessible forms, which is something like an endless circular series of "Who?"s, ultimately leading to what seems to be like a kind of infinite regression back into the boundless source of consciousness itself.

42

A Woman Comes Out of Absorption

In ancient times, Manjushri went to an assembly of Buddhas. When the other Buddhas returned to their respective domains, a woman remained, sitting near Gautama Buddha, in a state of absorption.

Manjushri said to Buddha, "Why can a woman sit near Buddha, when I cannot?"

Buddha said to Manjushri, "All you have to do is wake the woman up, get her out of absorption, and ask her yourself."

Manjushri circled the woman three times and snapped his fingers. Then he lifted her up to pure heaven, using all of his spiritual powers, but was not able to get her out of absorption.

Buddha said, "Even a hundred thousand Manjushris could not get this woman out of absorption. Below here, past as many worlds as grains of sand in twelve trillion Ganges Rivers, there is a bodhisattva named Ensnared Light who can get this woman out of absorption."

In a moment, the great being Ensnared Light sprang up from the earth and bowed to Buddha. Buddha instructed Ensnared Light to go up to the woman and snap his fingers once. When he did so, the woman emerged from absorption.

WUMEN SAYS,

Buddha acted out a complex play, having nothing in common with minor trivia.

Now tell me: Manjushri was the teacher of seven Buddhas; why couldn't he get the woman out of absorption? Ensnared Light was a bodhisattva of the first stage; why was he able to get her out?

If you can see intimately here, you will attain the great dragonic absorption even in the flurry of active consciousness.

WUMEN'S VERSE

Whether or not they can get her out,
She has attained freedom.
With a spirit head and a ghost face,
Defeat amounts to elegance.

ZEN MASTER ZHENJING'S VERSE

Buddha-nature is a natural reality;
Who says there is any other teacher?
Where Ensnared Light snapped his fingers,
When the woman came out of meditation,
Not the slightest effort was expended—
When were thoughts ever stirred?
Living beings are all equal;
They produce many doubts and obstacles by themselves,
in the course of their daily activities.

ZEN MASTER LANGYA'S VERSE

The woman, Manjushri, and Ensnared Light:
Ultimately how do Zen followers understand?
Only if you harmonize subtly, beyond convention,
Will you believe the waves are basically water.

TRANSLATOR'S COMMENTS

Manjushri, a transhistorical bodhisattva, or enlightening being, is a central figure in Buddhist iconography and a sort of patron saint of Zen. Portrayed as an eternal youth, Manjushri represents formless knowledge of absolute truth.

The woman in the story represents total absorption in absolute truth and immersion in the quiescence of nirvana. Manjushri is unable to get her *out* of that state because it is none other than his own domain (ineffable knowledge of the absolute) in which she is absorbed. Indeed, as Buddha says in the story, "even a hundred thousand Manjushris could not get this woman out of absorption," because the absolute is the "zero point" of Zen, and a thousand times zero equals zero.

What the individual in this state needs is complementary experience and knowledge. The complement to nirvanic absorption in absolute truth is discerning knowledge of relative truth, represented in this koan by the bodhisattva Ensnared Light. The name Ensnared Light symbolizes consciousness and knowledge of the apparent world, or mind absorbed in matter.

These two kinds of knowledge, formless insight into absolute truth and discerning cognition of relative truth, are the basis for the two essential aspects of Buddhism, known as wisdom and compassion. The Way of Buddhahood is lived through the harmonious combination of these two fundamental qualities.

Wumen's prose comment begins by affirming the message of the koan that enlightenment is not just nirvana per se; that is why he says that Buddha "acted out" a "complex play." The point of the word "act" is that enlightenment is not just transcendental knowledge (represented by

Manjushri), but also practical knowledge (represented by Ensnared Light). The "complexity" of the play refers to knowledge of differentiations; it is called a "play" because it is carried on in the domain of relative truth.

Wumen also remarks that this "complex play" has nothing in common with "minor trivia." In the technical language of Zen, this means that the reality of this koan is not a ritual performance, not a mythological recital, and not an indication of literal belief in supernatural powers or supernal beings.

Wumen continues his prose comment with the usual distillation of a pivotal question, which he poses to the reader to bring the koan alive. In this case, the reason for the answer is obvious; the issue is in the actual application. Wumen says that if we can see "intimately," that is, in first-hand experience, we will attain "the great dragonic absorption" even in the "flurry of active consciousness."

"The great dragonic absorption" is a Buddhist technical term for a state of mind undisturbed in the midst of the mundane world. This is called "dragonic" because in Buddhist iconography a dragon is considered to be in a very lofty state of trance in spite of being in the body of an animal, which is regarded as a comparatively low estate in the evolutionary scale. In saying that this is attained even in the midst of the flurry of ordinary activities of consciousness, Wumen simply makes this aspect of the definition of this state of mind explicit to the reader.

Wumen's verse comment is very clever, turning things around to call attention to two of the profoundest and most subtle points of attention in Buddhist meditation. The first point is the inclusion of relative reality within absolute reality; whatever relative reality may be, or however it may be described, it is enveloped and pervaded by absolute reality. The second point is the essence of the absoluteness of absolute reality; although the absolute pervades everything relative, nothing relative is itself absolute.

The first two lines of the verse characterize the experience of emptiness as pivotal. This means that one who has this perspective is not bound to any point of view, be it that of nirvana or that of samsara, that of absolute truth or that of relative truth. True adepts can experience nirvana and samsara simultaneously, yet demonstrate or emphasize one or the other expediently for the sake of edifying others.

In the last two lines Wumen also rescues literal-minded readers from the temptation to believe that the woman in this koan is an object of censure or ridicule. Her "spirit head" was her profound experience of nirvana; her "ghost face" was her immediate response to samsara. Her "defeat" refers on one level to absorption in nirvana, which was perfect in its profundity, as symbolized by the fact that Manjushri could not move her. Her "defeat" on another level refers to her awakening by Ensnared Light, which was perfect in its sensitivity, as symbolized by her instantaneous response. In both senses, "defeat amounts to elegance."

The lengthy verse comment of Zen master Zhenjing (pronounced Jun-jing) is most extraordinarily clear. It seems to me that any comment on it would spoil its unusual spiritual beauty; I can only suggest that readers look at it very closely and completely.

The verse of Zen master Langya is simple but contains one or two special expressions. He explicitly states that the point of the koan is to harmonize nirvana and samsara, or consciousness of absolute truth and consciousness of relative truth. To do so "subtly" means to be able to integrate these two levels of awareness simultaneously, rather than merely go through an intermittent alternation of disparate states.

This harmonization is "beyond convention" in that the conceptual boundaries between samsara and nirvana dissolve. Only then, Langya concludes, will one realize that the "waves" of relative reality are in essence not separate from the "water" of absolute reality. In other terms, the "waves" of knowledge of differentiation are not separated from the "water" of the oceanic consciousness of unity.

43

The Bamboo Stick

Master Shoushan held up a bamboo stick before a group and said, "If you call it a bamboo stick, you are clinging. If you do not call it a bamboo stick, you are ignoring. So tell me, what do you call it?"

WUMEN SAYS,
Call it a bamboo stick, and you're clinging. Don't call it a bamboo stick, and you're ignoring. You cannot say anything, yet you cannot say nothing. Speak quickly! Speak quickly!

WUMEN'S VERSE
Picking up a bamboo stick,
He enforces a life and death order:
With clinging and ignoring neck and neck,
Buddhas and Zen masters beg for their lives.

ZEN MASTER MINGZHAO PU SAID,
Had I been there at the time, when he said, "What do you call it?" I would have simply whistled a couple of times and watched old Shoushan crumble and melt.

ZEN MASTER SI-AN'S VERSE

Not clinging, yet not ignoring,
It is useless to bother initiating deliberation;
If you open your mouth and go on discussing further,
White clouds cover thousands of miles.

ZEN MASTER WAN-AN'S VERSE

Reviling others is reviling yourself;
Anger at others is anger at yourself.
Be wary of this, be careful;
What comes from you returns to you.

TRANSLATOR'S COMMENTS

Zen master Shoushan (pronounced Sho-shahn) lived in the tenth century. He was the successor to Fengxue, who was met with in koan number twenty-four, "Detachment from Words." In his time, Fengxue was the last living master of the Linji lineage of Zen; his successor Shoushan began a dramatic revival of the Zen school upheld by this lineage. This koan of Shoushan's was a favorite device of the later Linji master Dahui, a spiritual descendant of Shoushan who was also a major figure in yet another revitalization of Zen teaching.

The question of how to avoid both clinging and ignoring is equivalent to the pragmatic issue of combining consciousness of absolute truth with consciousness of relative truth, or how to combine wisdom and compassion. As mentioned before, the Indian Zen ancestor Nagarjuna wrote about absolute "emptiness" in a famous collection of verses on the Middle Way of balance and harmony: "Emptiness wrongly viewed destroys the feeble-minded, like a mishandled serpent or misapplied spell." He also wrote, "It has been said by the Victorious that emptiness is departure from all views; but those who keep the view of emptiness are called incurable."

Therefore when someone clings to a habitual compulsion to label and define everything in conventionally fixed terms ("call it a stick"), this is called attachment to views. By this expression Zen Buddhists do not just mean intellectual or emotional attachments to certain ways of looking at things, they also mean the whole complex of behavioral syndromes that accompany such attachments, such as materialism, aggression, and conceit.

Those who practice Zen learn to stop compulsively trying to label and define everything in fixed terms, detaching from conceptually construed truths in order to see into ineffable absolute truth. As for the Zen master's saying that you are ignoring if you do not call it a bamboo stick, this contains two meanings. In one sense, insight into ultimate reality is called ignorance of superficial appearances; in another sense, denial of any reality is called ignorance of actual fact. Thus in his prose comment Wumen says "You cannot say anything, yet you cannot say nothing." It is necessary to be the host of both emptiness and existence.

Wumen's verse comment describes the pivotal question in this koan as a "life and death order," which is meant both literally and symbolically. Do not cling to superficialities, and the habit of clinging to superficialities dies out. When the habit of clinging to superficialities dies out, the capacity for deep insight comes to life. Don't ignore the objective reality of suchness, and the habit of heedlessness dies out. When the habit of heedlessness dies out, the capacity for discerning awareness comes to life.

The final lines of Wumen's verse symbolize the complete integration of the relative ("clinging") and the absolute ("ignoring"), and indicate that this is an essential realization for all enlightened people.

Turning to the comments and verses of other Zen masters, the "whistle" of Mingzhao Pu (pronounced Ming-djow Poo) symbolizes the integration of absolute and conventional truths in a concrete act, insofar as it is articulated (thereby representing conventional truth), yet in a sense not articulate (thereby representing absolute truth.)

The verse of Zen master Si-an (pronounced Sih-ahn) reminds the reader that this koan is not an intellectual conundrum to be solved by an exercise of linear thought.

The verse of Zen master Wan-an looks like a moralistic truism, and works well enough on that level. Its technical meaning is that whatever thoughts and ideas you project on suchness are in actual fact the limitations you yourself impose on your own mind. This is the self-inhibiting mechanism underlying vicious circles and deadening habits of thought and behavior. The essential purpose of Zen is to free the mind from these unnecessary limitations, to restore the pristine innocence and autonomy of the enlightened nature in everyone.

44

The Staff

Master Baqiao said to a group, "If you have a staff, I will give you a staff; if you have no staff, I will take your staff away."

WUMEN SAYS,
It helps you across a river where the bridges are out,
and gets you back to the village when there is no moon.
If you call it a staff, you go to hell fast as an arrow.

WUMEN'S VERSE
The depths and shallows everywhere
Are all within his grip:
Holding up the sky and bracing the earth,
Wherever he is he makes Zen flourish.

ZEN MASTER DAHUI'S VERSE
At the crossroads
he does business with what's at hand;
But if you want to haggle,
you stumble by in ignorance.

ZEN MASTER WUZHUO'S VERSE

Baqiao raised his staff,
Startling all creation:
Shrimp may fly past the heavens,
But eyebrows are still above eyes.

ZEN MASTER KENTANG'S VERSE

In a village where the wells are poisoned
The water should not even be tasted;
Even with a single drop of it
The whole family dies.

TRANSLATOR'S COMMENTS

Baqiao (pronounced Bah-chyow) was one of the last Zen masters of the subtle and lofty-minded school known as the Gui-Yang house because of its spiritual descent from the great masters Guishan (who appeared in koan forty) and Yangshan (who appeared in koan twenty-five).

This koan has many levels of meaning. One level of interpretation represents different aspects of the total Zen teaching. Part of the teaching deals with cause and effect relationships in the relative world. This is represented by the statement, "If you have a staff, I will give you a staff." Another part of the teaching deals with the vanity of conceptions about absolute reality in itself. This aspect of teaching is ordinarily phrased in a negative way, precisely because no concept of the absolute truth is objectively accurate. People are prone to misconstrue this apparent negativity and exaggerate it into nothingness, so the teacher abolishes the notion of nothingness in emptiness. This is represented by the statement, "If you have no staff, I will take your staff away." As the great Buddhist master Nagarjuna wrote, "Without relying on common usage, ultimate truth cannot be expressed; without going to ultimate truth, nirvana cannot be attained."

On another level, this koan refers to authentic understanding. Those who have some authentic understanding receive more from the source of all understanding; while those who have no authentic understanding are ultimately unable to hold on to their subjective conceptions.

A third level is seen by putting yourself in the place of the Zen master, who symbolizes individual autonomy. In whatever situation you may find yourself, whether to concede or deny, whether to be active or passive, whether to get involved or abstain, is entirely up to you.

In a deeper reflection of this same sense, the Zen master stands for consciousness itself. Since the experienced world is a relationship between the perceiver and the perceived, for each individual subject the issue of what "is" or "isn't" depends on that individual's consciousness and perception.

In Wumen's comments, the "staff" is mind. The verses of the other Zen masters illustrate how to use this story to stay in centered balance and how to clear the mind of bias and partiality. This is especially clear in the last verse by Kentang (pronounced Kun-tahng), who warns us not to kill our living awareness of the vast panorama of being-as-is by imbibing false ideas and partial judgments.

45

Who Is That?

Wuzu said, "The past and future Buddhas are servants of another. Tell me, who is that?"

WUMEN SAYS,
If you can see that one clearly, it will be like bumping
into your own father at a crossroads; you don't have to
ask anyone else whether or not that's the one.

WUMEN'S VERSE
Don't draw another's bow,
Don't ride another's horse,
Don't discuss others' errors,
Don't mind others' business.

ZEN MASTER YE-NIU SAID,
The past and future Buddhas are servants of another; do Zen
followers past and present know, or not? Where the wine is
fine, you don't need to hang up a sign; where the vinegar's
sharp, why put up a gourd?

ZEN MASTER NANTANG'S VERSE

Old in years, the season late,
Pleasurable things far away,
It's not like childhood days
When you didn't know how to be sad.

TRANSLATOR'S COMMENTS

Here is Zen master Wuzu again with his pesky questions. The "past and future Buddhas" represent the means by which people attain enlightenment and the means by which people transmit enlightenment. The "Buddha of the Past" stands for the teachings that lead the individual to personal liberation from past limitations, and thus to awakening of preexisting potential. The "Buddha of the Future" stands for teachings formulated in the aftermath of enlightenment for the purpose of communicating with others in new situations yet to come in the future.

Zen master Wuzu asks us to look into the root of the whole matter: Who is the master of the past and future Buddhas? There is no practical use in giving the obvious answer, that it is the universal Buddha-nature or Buddha-mind. The question of the koan is precisely the fundamental question of Zen that everyone who seeks enlightenment has to ask inwardly.

Wumen cannot stress this enough in his prose and verse comments, where he reminds us over and over again that the essential study of Buddhism is the study of the essence of mind, carried out by internal investigation of one's own experience of consciousness, and not by concern with irrelevant externals.

The comments of Zen masters Ye-niu (pronounced Yeh-nyu) and Nantang take interesting turns in order to make sure the reader does not mistake a shallow understanding for a deep realization.

Ye-niu speaks of the liberated essence of mind, which is also called the host, or the master. When this essence is fully liberated ("fine wine"), there is no need to cling to the letter of expedient doctrine ("hang up a sign"). When the essence is fully awakened ("sharp vinegar"), there is no need to advertise ("put up a gourd"). This artful Zen statement also cautions seekers not to mistake intellectual or emotional self-consciousness ("sign," "gourd") for authentic perception of the essence of mind ("wine," "vinegar").

As for Nantang's doleful verse, the least of its lessons is that we shouldn't let melancholy stop us from learning. What we learn at such times may be precisely that which will teach us how to be master of emotions rather than be mastered by emotions.

In its strict technical sense, in contrast, this verse is extraordinarily artful and indirect, both reinforcing the first meaning and adding further dimension. In these four brief lines, Nantang basically says that true wakefulness of the liberated essential mind is nothing like ideas and sentiments of the ego, which is conditioned from childhood onward and therefore naively assumed to be real or true. In practical terms, this means that we need to see beyond, or beneath, the various artificial selves we have acquired and developed through the formation of psychological habits, in order to arrive at the underlying self of selves.

 46

Stepping Forward
Atop a Pole

Master Shishuang said, "Atop a hundred-foot pole, how do you step forward?"

Another ancient worthy said, "One who sits atop a hundred-foot pole may have gained initiation, but this is not yet reality. Atop a hundred-foot pole, one should step forward to manifest the whole body throughout the universe."

WUMEN SAYS,
If you can step forward and flip around, what more aversion is there to any place as unworthy of honor?

Now tell me, at the top of a hundred-foot pole, how do you step forward? Whoops!

WUMEN'S VERSE
If you blind the eye on top,
Mistakenly sticking to the zero point of the scale,
Giving up your body, you can abandon your life,
But you'll be one blind leading many blind.

TRANSLATOR'S COMMENTS

Zen master Shishuang (pronounced Shir-shwong) was one of the great masters of the classical era, known for his establishment of a "dead tree hall" where Zen seekers plunged into nirvana. He is therefore a perfect icon for this koan, which has to do with gaining a higher balance after the experience of nirvana, here symbolized by the top of a pole.

One of the most important scriptures of Buddhist psychology and meditation is called *The Discourse on Unlocking the Mysteries*. This highly developed and unusually subtle and detailed text explains the relationships among absolute, relative, and imagined reality. One of its most important revelations is the technical description of "tranquil nirvana" as "the highest expedient." In other words, nirvana is the highest expedient for seeing through the deceptions of imagined truth to the realities of objective truth.

The *Lotus Scripture*, another important Buddhist text already mentioned, describes tranquil nirvana as an "illusory citadel," which is expediently represented as ultimate relief in order to soothe the fears of those who face the endless infinity of the path of real being-as-is.

The present koan and Wumen's comments drive home the point that nirvana is not in itself the goal of Zen Buddhism, but a temporary resting place on an endless pathway of complete realization. Wumen's prose comment first describes the shift in attention from the peace of nirvana to the infinity of suchness, then observes the essential equality of all phenomena when they are seen as just "such."

Then, lest the reader remain complacently or indiscriminately in mirrorlike awareness as though it were the sum of Zen, or fall into the notion that the totality of real suchness

202

is an undifferentiated unity, Wumen concludes with a typical Zen question to engage the required attention: *How* do you step forward? It is no coincidence that one of the most popular Zen proverbs for this situation can be read to say, "Watch your step!" or "See right where you are!" This is being "not blind to causality."

One of the main problems with jumping to conclusions about Zen is represented by the distinction made here by Wumen. It is not just "that" you emerge from nirvana to higher integration; it is also "how" you do it. Sometimes people who emerge from nirvana precipitately, without considering this "how," become mentally unstable or even deranged. This is one source of the eccentricity known in technical literature as "crazy Zen."

Wumen's verse comment summarizes the danger of overestimating the experience of quiescent nirvana and mistaking a means for the end. Slightly more concealed is the parallel message that there are counterfeit and genuine versions of nirvana. It is not only the counterfeit nirvana (quietism or nihilism) that "blinds" the unwary seeker, but even the real nirvana also blinds people when it is taken out of context as an expedient method and turned into an object of devotion as if it were an ultimate goal.

47

Three Barriers

Master Tushuai Yue set up three barriers to question students:

1) Brushing aside confusion to search out the hidden is only for the purpose of seeing essence. Right now where is your essence?
2) Only when you know your own essence can you be freed from birth and death. When you are dying, how will you be free?
3) When you are freed from birth and death, then you will know where you are going. When the elements disintegrate, where do you go?

WUMEN SAYS,
If you can utter three pivotal sayings here, you can be the master wherever you are; whatever circumstances you encounter are themselves the source.

Otherwise, it is easy to fill up on coarse food, hard to starve if you chew thoroughly.

WUMEN'S VERSE
In an instant of thought, survey measureless eons;
The affairs of measureless eons are the very present.
Right now see through this instant of thought,
And you see through the person now seeing.

TRANSLATOR'S COMMENTS

Tushuai Yue (pronounced Too-shwai Yweh) was one of the later masters of the Linji school of Zen. This school generally showed a proclivity for systematic koan construction such as demonstrated here.

The exercise presented here may be summarized as follows:

1) Stand aside from the rustle of thoughts to try to see into the essential mind.

2) Maintain independent awareness of the essential mind when thoughts die out. Note that there is a tendency for part of the mind to start up in fear when reaching the brink of nirvana. The habit-ridden psyche then pours forth images, ideas, and thoughts, thus distracting attention from the absolute and thereby retreating from the overwhelming power of nirvanic experience, which is so threatening to the limited ego.

This last-minute psychic flurry is a common theme in Buddhist iconography and mythology, because it actually does happen to almost everyone. Many people in deep meditation do become agitated or frightened at the eleventh hour, on the verge of the

"Great Death" of the false self, thus spoiling the result. Tushuai zeros in on this critical point in the transformation of consciousness, asking, "When you are 'dying,' how will you be free?"

3) Once you get through confusion and distraction to attain the nirvanic calm of the original mind and are freed from bondage to coming and going thoughts and feelings (samsara, or "birth and death"), then you will know real suchness. When the "elements" of mentally constructed versions of reality "disintegrate" (as a result of the foregoing process of Zen concentration), your future lies in your own relationship with the reality of suchness as it is.

Wumen's prose comment begins by affirming that when you succeed in this exercise, you can remain in contact with your basic mind, regardless of what may go through your head or what may take place around you. If you have not yet understood, he gives another description.

"It is easy to fill up on coarse food" symbolizes plunging into nirvana, or resorting to the mirrorlike awareness of everything at once. As a matter of fact, each of these (nirvana and mirrorlike awareness), when properly carried out as an exercise, leads to knowledge of the other one as an experience.

"It is hard to starve if you chew thoroughly" symbolizes complete integration of two aspects of Zen: 1) insight into the basis of consciousness; and 2) everyday management of the actions and products of consciousness. The expression "chew thoroughly" also represents thorough knowledge of the differentiations in suchness. In this case also, each meaning of the line represents an exercise that completes the experience of the other.

Wumen's verse summarizes a way of practicing the koan:

1) Observe the constant essence of mind underlying its fluctuating functions.
2) Use the insight thus fostered to unify formerly fragmentary perception of being-as-is.
3) Use this extradimensional perspective to see through subjectivity in perception.
4) By seeing through subjectivity, realize the objective nature of the self.

48

One Road

A monk asked Master Qianfeng, " 'The Blessed Ones of the ten directions have one road of nirvana.' Where is the road?"

Qianfeng raised his staff, drew a line, and said, "Here."

Subsequently the monk asked Master Yunmen for further instruction. Yunmen held up a fan and said, "This fan leaps up to the thirty-third heaven and bumps into the nose of the chief of the celestial rulers; the carp of the eastern sea are given a blow, and it rains buckets."

WUMEN SAYS,

One sifts dirt and raises dust on the bottom of the deepest sea; one rouses waves and floods the sky at the top of the highest mountain. Holding still, letting go, each puts forth a single hand to help set up a way to the source. It was very much like two racers bumping into each other. In all the world there could be no one who matches up, but from the point of view of the absolute eye, even those two great elders did not know the road at all.

WUMEN'S VERSE
You've already arrived before you take a step:
It's already explained before a word is said.
Even if you keep on top of the situation with every move,
Still you should know there's an opening higher beyond.

ZEN MASTER HUANGLONG NAN SAID,
Qianfeng temporarily pointed out a road, bending over backward for a beginner. Yunmen communicated the evolution, to get later people not to weary.

ZEN MASTER FOJIAN'S VERSE
One man rides a boat across dry land,
One man rides a horse on a needle point:
They arrive at the Capital at the same time, same day,
But one of them was most sharply focused.

TRANSLATOR'S COMMENT

Qianfeng (pronounced Chyen-fung) was a distinguished master of the same school as Caoshan, who appears in koan number ten, "Alone and Poor." Yunmen, who has already been seen in several koans, spent time studying the subtleties of Zen with both elder masters Caoshan and Qianfeng after his own enlightenment.

The koan at hand illustrates what Indian Buddhists called the Ekayana (pronounced Eh-kuh-yaa-nuh), which means One Vehicle. This term refers to the total scope of the essence and function of Buddhism as a science of human liberation. Technically speaking, the One Vehicle may be viewed from two perspectives, one that is perceptible to all people and therefore is called "common," and another that is perceptible only to people at a certain stage of awareness and therefore is called "special."

Simple as this principle of classification seems, some of the most sophisticated problems of Buddhist psychology and philosophy revolve around it. My purpose in mentioning the two visions of One Vehicle here is not to introduce a learned discourse on this subject, but to alert readers to a "barb" in the unconscious temptation to suppose that the two cannot be at once different and equal, that one must be better than the other.

In terms of Buddhist systems, this koan and the riddle of the two "One Vehicles" can be illustrated in terms of Flower Ornament Buddhism, which is based on the Buddhist text known as the *Flower Ornament Scripture;* and in terms of Lotus Buddhism, which is based on the Buddhist text known as the *Lotus Scripture.*

In the terms of Flower Ornament Buddhism, one Zen master illustrates the perspective of "all in one," seeing everything at once as one integral whole; the other Zen master illustrates the perspective of "one in all," seeing the unity of everything in the whole of its plurality. If these seem to be exactly the same to you, or if they seem completely different, now you know the reason for this koan. Both of these facets of total perception are necessary for complete mentation; yet because they are interdependent, neither of them is an absolute basis. This is why Wumen delivers the Zen coup de grace at the close of his prose and verse comments, turning the attention to the ineffable source of the one and the all.

In the terms of the *Lotus Scripture,* one Zen master points to the ineffable transcendence of quiescent nirvana, another hints at the infinite livingness of suchness. There is suchness in Qianfeng's quiescent nirvana, which he indicates is anywhere and therefore everywhere; and there is quiescent nirvana in Yunmen's suchness, as he demonstrates how even the most unexpected and extravagant happenings cannot disturb the unity of his vision and the equanimity of his observation.

Wumen's prose comment begins with an excellent description of these multiple *entendres*, using traditional Zen symbolism. Then he turns our attention to ourselves, to see if we are only partially awake, "leaning to one side." Wumen wants us to open our "absolute eye," which can see the One Road in both its totality and its particulars, without either mode of awareness domineering over the other, and without their interplay obstructing the more fundamental or essential consciousness of the basic mind.

Wumen begins his verse comment by depicting the omnipresence of the ineffable absolute. He goes on to say that if you use subtle awareness of this omnipresent absolute in order to clear your mind of superficial thoughts, that will allow you to attain intimacy with suchness. The final line contains multiple warnings, which may be summarized as follows:

1) Don't let absorption in the silence of nirvana cause you to forget the essence of mind.
2) Don't let fascination with the infinity of suchness cause you to forget the essence of mind.
3) Don't let the ongoing task of coordinating the heart of nirvana and the knowledge of differentiation cause you to forget the essence of mind.

Here again Wumen skillfully evokes Yunmen's style of Zen expression, renowned for its subtlety and ability to contain three statements within every remark. One of the criteria I use to evaluate Zen masters after the classical era is their ability to express this sort of versatility and depth without simply imitating others. This would express the freedom of the Zen mind more than literary poetic sentiment, or the routine habit of turning everything into cliché.

The remark of Huanglong on this koan presents an exact description of the main outline of Lotus Buddhism. The first line stresses the point that quiescent nirvana is a temporary expedient; the second line hints at the infinite endlessness of suchness.

In schools of Chinese Buddhism inheriting the Lotus tradition, quiescent nirvana is called the magical castle, the illusory citadel, the temporary abode, with all these terms referring to its expedient nature. The endless experience of working consciously with suchness, in contrast, is called the continent of jewels, the knowledge of all knowledge, and the vision and cognition of Buddhahood.

Finally, the verse of master Fojian symbolically describes the integration of the heart of nirvana with objective knowledge of the world, indicating the different approaches of the two masters as well as the different ways in which each master's approach can be viewed. Lest we be confused by difference in approach and imagine this means difference in destination, Fojian says they "arrive in the Capital at the same time, same day."

Still fearing vagueness in understanding, Fojian cautions us that there is orderly procedure involved in the work of integrating different modes of consciousness. It is not an arbitrarily forced mixture based on the subconscious notion that we can gain access to the actual experience of integrated awareness simply by having the idea that it can be done.

In plain terms, there have always been people, especially intellectuals, who demand more enlightenment than they can actually perceive, let alone sustain, because they are overly impressed by the theoretical knowledge they have of its existence. People like this often have to unlearn a lot before they can find out what is real.

It may appear here that Fojian is saying one or the other of the Zen masters was "most sharply focused." It may also seem that he is saying one way of interpreting each Zen master's pointer is "most sharply focused." It may also be evident that the sharpest focus is on the specific needs and capacities of the individual at a given stage on the Way. The One Road of Nirvana is anywhere and everywhere, but your journey begins from right where you are.

Now where are *you*? To focus this question "most sharply," place before yourself the questions it contains. Where is *who*? Which *who* or *you* is there? *Who* says *where* or *there*?

About the Translator

Thomas Cleary has studied Zen koans for thirty years, and has long been acknowledged worldwide as a master translator of Zen texts. His acclaimed translations of Buddhist and Taoist classics, renowned for their unusual lucidity, have been adopted as international standards for retranslation into French, Dutch, German, Italian, Portuguese, Spanish, and Turkish.

The new accessibility of Eastern ideas through Dr. Cleary's expert translations has extended their audience beyond the cultural fringes of Western civilization to the vanguard of modern thinking in science, education, business, and diplomacy.